UNEXPECTED POWER

SHAREEN HERTEL

UNEXPECTED POWER

Conflict and Change among Transnational Activists

ILR Press an imprint of
CORNELL UNIVERSITY PRESS
Ithaca and London

Portions of this book are based on the article "New Moves in Transnational Advocacy: Getting Labor and Economic Rights on the Agenda in Unexpected Ways," *Global Governance: A Review of Multilateralism and Humane Governance* 12, no. 3. Copyright © 2006 by Lynne Rienner Publishers. Used with permission.

First published 2006 by Cornell University Press
First printing, Cornell Paperbacks, 2006

Printed in the United States of America

Library of Congress Cataloging-in-Publication Data

Hertel, Shareen.
   Unexpected power : conflict and change among transnational activists / Shareen Hertel.
      p. cm.
   Includes bibliographical references and index.
   ISBN-13: 978-0-8014-4507-1 (cloth : alk. paper)
   ISBN-10: 0-8014-4507-8 (cloth : alk. paper)
   ISBN-13: 978-0-8014-7324-1 (pbk. : alk. paper)
   ISBN-10: 0-8014-7324-1 (pbk. : alk. paper)
   1. Human rights—Cross-cultural studies. 2. Human rights—Societies, etc. 3. Pressure groups—Cross-culture studies.   I. Title.
   JC571.H443 2006
   322.4'3—dc22
                                          2006014455

Cloth printing   10 9 8 7 6 5 4 3 2 1

Paperback printing   10 9 8 7 6 5 4 3 2 1

For Donald

Contents

Acknowledgments

Many people have helped make this book possible. At Columbia University, Douglas Chalmers, Mark Kesselman, Robert Kaufman, Victoria Murillo, Andrew Nathan, Thomas Pogge, Jack Snyder, and Charles Tilly as well as members of the University Seminar on Human Rights and the University Seminar on Globalization all commented on various portions of the manuscript, for which I am grateful. Rainer Braun, Paola Cesarini, Scott Martin, and Ray Smith commented on related work, while Dawn Brancati and Miguel Carter have read and edited countless drafts of chapters. I am indebted to them all.

Also at Columbia, the Department of Political Science and the Graduate School of Arts and Sciences afforded me grants for study, summer research, and conference travel; the Institute of Latin American Studies in conjunction with the Tinker Foundation supported my summer research in Mexico; and the Center for the Study of Human Rights awarded me funding though a Gitelson-Meyerowitz Essay Award for work that eventually became part of chapter 4. I acknowledge all of this support gratefully. I was also fortunate to have excellent research assistance from Evann Smith and Seth Rosenfeld at Columbia.

I am grateful to colleagues at both El Colegio de la Frontera Norte (Tijuana) and El Colegio de Sonora (Hermosillo) for the research and administrative support I received while a visiting scholar at both of those Mexican universities in 2001, and to José Luis Anguiano and Leonor Cedillo for their logistical support in Tijuana and Hermosillo, respectively.

At the University of Connecticut, my colleagues in the Department of Political Science and the Human Rights Institute have been extremely supportive of my efforts to shape this manuscript into a book. Mark Boyer, Richard Hiskes, Peter Kingstone, Howard Reiter, Evelyn Simien, and Richard Wilson have all commented on related writing and research or advised me on the production of the book. Darren Favello provided excellent research support. Jennifer Fontanella, Justine Hill, and Rachel Jackson have provided critical administrative support. The University of Connecticut Research Foundation has provided financial support related to final production of the manuscript.

At ILR Press/Cornell University Press, Fran Benson enthusiastically supported this project. Together with Nancy Ferguson, Karen Hwa, and others, she moved the manuscript through the editorial and production processes in record time.

This book would not have been possible without the hundreds of hours of interviews carried out with people in the United States, Mexico, and Bangladesh. Behind every interview is a story: not only that of the person with whom I spoke, but also that of the person who gave me each contact. I acknowledge in particular Ruth Borgman, Linda Dworak-Muñoz, Judy Gearhart, Ricardo Hernández, Ed Krueger, Ruth Rosenbaum, Robert Smith, and Arturo Sotomayor for their invaluable introductions to people in Mexico; and Sajeda Amin, Kelly Askin, Sumaira Chowdhury, Rounaq Jahan, Roger Muchnick, Shakil Quazi, Rick Santos, Sunil Thadani, and Sufia Uddin for contacts in Bangladesh.

I am grateful for the precious time afforded me by the many representatives of nongovernmental organizations interviewed during their busy days, and by the workers I met with by the dozens. I especially wish to thank Julia Quiñónez of El Comité Fronterizo de Obreras (Piedras Negras, Mexico) for her willingness to begin a dialogue in the earliest stages of my research and for her continuing solidarity.

Finally, my husband, Donald Swinton, has believed in me, supported me, edited my work, and cheered me on. This book is dedicated to him. Our daughter, Jo, will have to wait for the next one.

UNEXPECTED POWER

New Dynamics in
Transnational Advocacy
An Introduction

Frans Ingelberts is an enigma: a Catholic lay missionary born in the heart of Europe, he lives in a modest, concrete block home on a rutted street in a poor neighborhood of Piedras Negras, Mexico, a dusty town just over the Mexican border from Eagle Pass, Texas. He runs a homeopathic drugstore of sorts, a small dispensary in the front room of the house he shares with his Mexican wife and family. And he is a community activist, involved in grassroots organizing on labor rights and community development. As Ingelberts, a wiry man in his fifties, chats with me and several Mexican labor rights activists at dusk one evening, he is full of quiet passion for his work, sardonic humor about United States–Mexico relations, and pain at the condition of life for people in places like Piedras Negras. This is a manufacturing town where workers make the T-shirts, toasters, and car parts that help clothe, feed, and move other people around the globe—yet barely earn enough to keep themselves from slipping backward further into poverty.

I ask about his views on the problem of pregnancy screening in the *maquiladoras*, the export-oriented manufacturing facilities that cluster in this and other dusty border towns. Ingelberts acknowledges the problem— but points beyond this most obvious form of gender discrimination to the deeper patterns of inequality that run through his own society and through the relationship between two vastly unequal neighboring countries. I came to talk with Ingelberts about gender discrimination in the *maquiladoras*— and leave as night falls, talking about social injustice and economic rights.

It is a pattern that will repeat throughout the discussions that form the human backdrop to this book. Subtly, as in this interview—and more overtly, in others—local activists turn the conversation to spotlight the issues they are most concerned about in the human rights sphere—not necessarily the issues outside observers would place at the top of the list of priorities for action. By moving beneath the surface of cross-border campaigns to explore the differences in how activists perceive and prioritize rights, this book opens up new ways to interpret transnational advocacy and norms evolution. It draws on hundreds of hours' worth of interviews with people like Frans Ingelberts—frontline participants in human rights struggles in developing countries, who played a key role in bringing economic rights to the fore of human rights advocacy in the 1990s.

Fair trade, child labor, discrimination against women in the workplace: during the "sweatshop decade" (as the 1990s were commonly referred to in the media), issues like these were the focus of a series of high-profile transnational advocacy campaigns.[1] The activists who organized such campaigns often did so in the name of human rights. Yet how broadly or narrowly did they define those rights? And how, if at all, did such normative[2] understandings of human rights change over the course of a campaign? What are the implications of change in human rights norms for academic scholarship, policy reform—and the lives of abused workers and poor people?

This book explores contemporary advocacy on labor and economic rights, analyzing the process of norms evolution within specific campaigns[3] and developing a strategic analysis of the way human rights claims are framed.[4] It proceeds in three stages: first, the book explains why and how two key mechanisms central to transnational advocacy emerge; second, it explores how actors involved in two specific advocacy campaigns employed such mechanisms to influence the evolution of normative understandings in those campaigns; and third, it assesses the effect of these campaigns on concrete policy outcomes.

The cases at the heart of the book—a transnational campaign to prevent child labor in Bangladesh, and one to prevent gender discrimination in the Mexican workplace—are two of the highest-profile examples of cross-border advocacy on labor and economic rights in the 1990s. Like other campaigns of the era, these campaigns involved consumers, members of labor unions, and representatives of nongovernmental organizations (NGOs) in coordinated activities aimed at exposing human rights abuses and demanding reform.

Yet these two cases are unique because in each, the very people these campaigns were intended to help—those on the "receiving end" of the

campaign, people like Frans Ingelberts—challenged the way that the or-
ganizers of each campaign defined human rights as well as the corresponding policy priorities of the campaign. This tug-of-war over meaning (in the one case overt, and in the other, more subtle) is the focus of
the book. Why and how did it take place? And what impact did it have
on policy outcomes, if any?

Founding scholarly work on transnational advocacy acknowledged
that conflicts *within* networks were a potentially significant source of
political change. As Margaret Keck and Kathryn Sikkink explained:
"[F]rame disputes can be a significant source of change within networks. . . . Western human rights norms have indeed been the defining
framework for many networks, but how these norms are articulated is
transformed in the process of network activity. . . . Modern networks are
not conveyor belts of liberal ideals, but vehicles for communicative and
political exchange, with the potential for mutual transformation of participants."[5] This book takes up such mutual transformation centrally and
systematically, showing how intranetwork conflict—over resources and
political access[6] as well as ideas—affects not only the evolution of
transnational advocacy itself but also norms change more broadly.

The book offers two new mechanisms to help explain why and how
actors on the receiving end of campaigns put forward alternative understandings of human rights norms. These mechanisms are the building
blocks of theory.[7] The book explores factors that influence their emergence and lays out a framework for understanding how the mechanisms
function, based on in-depth, inductive analysis of the cases at hand. The
aim is to introduce these new mechanisms to the rich and burgeoning
literature on transnational advocacy, norms evolution, and human
rights—in so doing, challenging prevailing interpretations of who sets
the "rights" agenda in transnational advocacy, while at the same time
paving the way for future and more broadly comparative theorizing.

The case studies central to this book, which scholar John Gerring
would describe as "disciplined configurative" case studies (as opposed
to either ideographic or nomothetic case studies), are developed so that
"each case is conceptualized as a unique combination of general factors—but not combinations that can be reduced to standardized variables in a general mode." The primary purpose of such disciplined configurative case studies, Gerring argues, is "to elucidate or confirm a
causal framework or mechanism rather than to verify a specific causal
proposition."[8] That is indeed the purpose of the case studies explored
here, and the larger intent of the book as a whole.

Understanding the Context

The end of communism in 1989 ushered in a decade of rapid geopolitical and economic integration. It also marked the end of a sharp East/West divide in human rights policymaking that had reinforced the distinction between different types of rights throughout the Cold War years, during which communist states gave priority to economic and social rights whereas capitalist states favored civil and political ones. During the 1990s, rapid expansion and diffusion of the internet, of electronic communications and media, and of global transportation links occurred. This was also an era of unprecedented networking among groups in civil society. Cybernetworks of activists, academics, and policy experts proliferated. The United Nations hosted a series of high-profile conferences to involve people from within civil society in debate over everything from the environment to population to human rights. And NGOs expanded their activity in industrialized and developing countries alike, worldwide.

As noted, the 1990s also bear the distinction of having been the "sweatshop years." The century that multiplied wealth more than any other in history closed having also multiplied income gaps more greatly than ever before.[9] As corporations found it easier to move manufacturing and service operations from industrialized to developing countries in search of lower wages (or to low-wage immigrant communities within industrialized countries), journalists and citizen groups could observe and monitor their activities more astutely. They could also share stories and images more widely with the public through expanded media outlets.

Likewise, as international trade and financial integration intensified, the risks of systemic shocks from crises in places like Mexico, Thailand, Brazil, and Russia increased. A public already concerned about the sweatshop scandals of celebrity endorsers such as Kathie Lee Gifford and corporations such as Nike angrily massed in Seattle during the 1999 World Trade Organization ministerial meetings to demand reforms in the global trade system that would diminish instability, increase equity, and enhance democratic participation in economic decision making.

Throughout this turbulent decade, new human rights rhetoric emerged as activists involved in protests over labor and economic issues began to phrase their demands for private- and public-sector reform in terms of human rights.[10] But these demands were not uniform—even within the same campaigns. Actors themselves involved in the campaigns often contested the scope and nature of the human rights at stake.

Were the rights at issue civil and political in nature or economic and social? Should activists emphasize the negative-rights dimensions of human rights (i.e., freedom from abuse) or the positive-rights dimensions (i.e., entitlement to particular goods or services)? Could they reconcile different priorities for action on the ground, given their differing access to resources and distinct understandings of the rights at stake?

This book highlights the differences in perspective—sometimes overt, other times more subtle—that emerged among activists involved the Bangladesh and Mexico campaigns, both within those countries and in countries from which the campaigns were launched. The book introduces two new mechanisms that help us explain how *less* materially or politically powerful activists within these networks managed to influence the way human rights were framed in each campaign. The case studies demonstrate that powerful actors within transnational networks do not always have the upper hand in setting the normative agenda. This counterintuitive finding adds complexity to the standard explanations of transnational advocacy and norms evolution.

Exploring the Mechanisms

Mechanisms are "frequently occurring and easily recognizable causal patterns . . . which allow us to explain, but not predict" events, according to Jon Elster.[11] Doug McAdam, Sidney Tarrow, and Charles Tilly define them as a "delimited class of events that alter relations among specified sets of elements in identical or closely similar ways over a variety of situations."[12] They are the building blocks of theory, useful in constructing partial explanations.[13] This book employs mechanisms to explain why particular understandings of norms emerge in the context of transnational advocacy and how they change over time as a result of these mechanisms.

Often activists who are better endowed with material resources and/or political capital assume that they can set the normative agenda of a given advocacy campaign. They "send" a particular human rights message, believing that those whom they are seeking to support through the campaign will "receive" the message, accept it, and collaborate with the "senders" to influence a given target through concrete actions such as boycotts or protest marches, for example.

However, the mechanisms developed in this book add a new dimension to the typical advocacy story: they enhance the ability of "receiving-end" activists to make alternative human rights claims. Both the normative frame of a campaign and the corresponding policy prescriptions and interpretation of norms beyond the campaign may shift as a result.

Blocking, the first mechanism introduced in the book, is action by receiving-end activists aimed at halting or at least significantly stalling a campaign's progress in order to pressure senders to change their frame. Activists on the receiving end of a campaign block by expressing norms in a way very distinct from that of the senders, seeking to stop the campaign until the understandings of norms on both "ends" of the campaign are aligned. Actors on the receiving end of the campaign choose normative reference points—such as human rights treaties—that are distinct from those the senders refer to in setting the campaign's opening frame. The receivers express their alternative position openly and use a variety of contentious tactics aimed at persuading the senders to change their frame and corresponding policy goals.

Backdoor moves, the second mechanism introduced in the book, are actions that receiving-end activists make aimed at augmenting a campaign's normative frame without stalling the campaign entirely. Receivers accept the normative reference points of senders—but they add distinct, secondary reference points and/or policy proposals. Backdoor moves are not openly conflictive and are often made indirectly.

Blocking and backdoor moves are not mutually exclusive; they can occur at different stages within the same campaign, and the same actors in a campaign may engage in both moves at different times. This book analyzes conditions under which activists choose to block, make backdoor moves, or employ mixed strategies—and the extent to which those strategic moves result in the overall advancement of new normative understandings and corresponding policy change in the context of contentious politics.[14]

Several factors influence the decision to block or make backdoor moves, including: (1) the manner in which a campaign emerges; (2) the nature of threats, if any, issued from the "sending" end of the campaign (such as sanctions); and (3) the degree to which receiving-end activists share an interest with senders in the overall success of a campaign. This book explores the interplay of these factors through detailed case study analysis.

In particular, it introduces two new forms of campaign evolution that provide alternatives to the explanation offered by Margaret Keck and Kathryn Sikkink, which has shaped much of the literature on transnational advocacy. Keck and Sikkink's pioneering work identified the "boomerang" pattern to explain the emergence of transnational advocacy campaigns: actors seek to change an oppressive situation in their own country by enlisting the help of external supporters; that help metaphorically "boomerangs" back via such campaigns.[15] This book identifies two new patterns of campaign emergence: an "outside-in" pattern and a "dual-target" pattern, which in turn affect the emergence of blocking and backdoor moves. These new forms of campaign evolution are discussed in depth in chapter 2 and illustrated through the succeeding case studies.

In addition, much of the existing literature on transnational advocacy focuses on the role of the actors who launch cross-border advocacy campaigns—"norms entrepreneurs" motivated by "altruism, empathy, [and] ideational commitment."[16] By contrast, this book focuses on the role of people who respond with alternative understandings to those posed by norms entrepreneurs.[17]

Several assumptions underlie the arguments developed in this book—the first being that a complex mixture of ideal[18] *and* material interests influences how actors behave in norm-centered endeavors (like advocacy campaigns). Their motives are not simply altruistic. Actors involved in campaigns on labor and economic rights—particularly actors on the receiving end of campaigns—care not only about making the world a better place. In many cases, they also care about ensuring their own economic survival and dignity in the workplace. Second, the pursuit of an object ends up transforming the object pursued: in several of the cases analyzed here, launching a campaign to pursue the fulfillment of certain norms ends up transforming the very norms themselves at stake.

The following is a brief illustration of how blocking and backdoor moves function in practice—specifically, in relation to the cases discussed in this book. Actors who *block* seek to halt a campaign entirely because the central human rights message does not resonate with their experience and understanding. In some cases, those blocking may at the same time propose new normative understandings and/or corresponding policy actions. In the Bangladesh case, for example, local activists on the receiving end of an anti-child-labor campaign sought to thwart that campaign's progress because they worried that the campaign would harm more than help local children—and that the campaign would have a devastating impact on the Bangladeshi economy as a whole. Receiving-end activists in Bangladesh thus blocked the U.S.-led campaign by denouncing it in the local and international press, while at the same time marshaling a countercampaign that highlighted the risks of removing children from the workplace without a viable alternative source of income. Simultaneously, the Bangladeshi activists proposed new ways of interpreting children's rights that took such economic rights more centrally into consideration.

By contrast, *backdoor moves* do not involve either overt disagreement over norms or actions aimed at stopping a campaign. Rather, there is the appearance of agreement on the central human rights message by both senders and receivers. Yet the receivers simultaneously introduce *additional* concepts and corresponding policy goals into the campaign's agenda. The end result may be to broaden the central normative message of the campaign beyond the senders' original scope—and to shift priorities for action on the ground as a consequence. In the Mexico case, for example, local Mexican activists accepted an antidiscrimination frame principally crafted by U.S.-based human rights activists, while at the same time broadening that message to include right-to-work and reproductive rights concerns. Rather than block, Mexican activists employed backdoor moves in an effort to defend these additional human rights. Some carried out grassroots outreach activities on economic rights along the United States–Mexico border, while others launched a "parallel campaign" from Mexico City, focused on reproductive rights.

The diagram below summarizes the effects of blocking and backdoor moves in the country case studies that follow. The impact of these mechanisms varies in terms of (1) the scope of change (i.e., blocking enables activists to demand a more expansive range of rights than do backdoor moves); and (2) the locus of change (i.e., blocking tends to result in shifts in normative discourse at the local, national, and/or transnational level, whereas backdoor moves tend to have more restricted impact, limited to the local level).

> **Bangladesh case:** blocking mechanism dominant → widens HR norm frame significantly (to include economic rights in transnational frame)
>
> **Mexico:** backdoor mechanism dominant → widens HR norm frame moderately (to include economic rights and reproductive rights in local-level frames *only*)

The campaigns discussed in this book involved expansive struggles for human rights in which receiving-end activists not only sought to put economic rights on an equal footing with civil and political rights but also highlighted the positive-rights dimensions of rights alongside the more typical, negative-rights ones. Theoretically, activists could also employ blocking or backdoor moves either to safeguard civil and political rights (the mainstay of much traditional human rights advocacy)[19] or to rein in a campaign's frame. This book does not take up such cases, but future scholars could do so, using the mechanisms introduced here as a starting point in their analysis.

What is most important to understand about blocking and backdoor moves is that they are mechanisms that centrally affect the evolution of normative understandings. They are not simply negative actions aimed at stalling or halting a campaign (or, by extension, norms evolution). Rather, they are mechanisms that complicate the first stage of norms evolution (the "emergence" phase), rendering it more complex than heretofore portrayed.

This book identifies the processes of social construction through which related normative understandings develop in the context of transnational advocacy, offering evidence of different types of motivation and strategic interaction among actors involved in these processes. It focuses on mechanisms (rather than covering laws, generalizable from a randomly selected population), given the nature of the subject matter: large-N datasets of transnational advocacy campaigns for labor and economic rights would be difficult to compile, given ongoing debate over the central organizing categories (i.e., what constitutes such a campaign?).[20] The book aims to create a framework for identifying significant patterns of interaction (i.e., mechanisms) that may appear in other political and social settings, thus paving the way for future large-scale data collection, analysis, comparison, and cumulative theorizing.[21]

Leading scholars have pioneered in identifying transnational networks and explaining the puzzle of why they emerge,[22] but they have spent less time exploring the material and normative differences *among actors within the same networks*. (Clifford Bob is an important exception, and his work is taken up in the next chapter.) The present book illustrates the normative complexities within advocacy networks, exploring how new human rights concerns (such as economic rights) emerge and can affect the outcomes of campaigns on the ground.

Reviewing the Scholarly Debates

The relationship between economic and labor rights and their connection, in turn, to human rights remain contested both theoretically and in practice. Leading international human rights scholar Philip Alston has characterized economic rights as "late starters" in the field. "[L]engthy debates" within the United Nations Commission on Human Rights over the past four decades, he argues, "have done very little to promote understanding of the core normative content of economic rights let alone the human rights dimensions of debt, world trade, and development cooperation."[23] Although economic and labor rights are codified in international instruments—from the International Covenant on Economic, Social and Cultural Rights[24] to the hundreds of labor conventions developed by the International Labour Organization (ILO)—the cases analyzed in this book reveal that there is not a widespread understanding of economic rights as core human rights.

Moreover, there is a considerable gap between norms on paper and norms in practice: even constitutionalized rights to health, shelter, work, education, or sanitation—among the most basic economic rights—are not always fulfilled effectively. And labor rights remain understood principally in civil and political terms, not economic and social ones, their negative dimensions more fully codified than their positive-rights ones. Thus the struggle to define the scope of human rights and corresponding remedies—particularly in relation to economic and labor rights—is a central aspect of both the Bangladesh and Mexico cases.

This book thus helps fill a significant gap in political science literature: existing literature on transnational advocacy tends to mirror the emphasis on the civil and political dimensions of human rights rather than emphasize economic or social rights aspects—particularly work on labor rights advocacy in the context of international trade debates.[25] (Analysis of recent antiglobalization protests is an important exception, as it has begun to introduce and elaborate upon the concept of economic rights.)[26] It contributes to debates in comparative politics on class and gender hierarchies between and among actors involved in social movements and transnational advocacy.[27] Actors who might otherwise be considered comparatively "weak" have new tools for getting their message out and for transforming the larger normative frame of a campaign if they block or make backdoor moves. In addition, the book addresses broader debates on the role of "global civil society"[28] in international relations, by exploring how notions of human rights differ among actors within this contested terrain and how those differences affect relations between states and multinational corporate actors.[29]

The book also engages the literature on norms—one of the most dynamic and contested subjects in political science and related disciplines, such as sociology. In political science, debates over norms straddle several critical ontological divides: the material versus the nonmaterial, rationalist versus constructivist.[30] The question of whether norms have independent causal force is intimately linked to larger agent/structure debates. How can we tell a norm when we see one? Are norms (like institutions, some would argue) merely epiphenomenal—lacking independent causal force and instead reflecting the distribution of power in the international system or within an individual state or society? What concrete evidence do we need to prove that a norm exists and to distinguish how it functions? The sources of norms themselves remain "ill-defined, incompletely theorized, and understudied"[31] in political science literature. This book identifies blocking and backdoor moves as key mechanisms in the process by which new normative understandings emerge in the context of transnational advocacy.

It also contributes to scholarly work on both social movements and transnational advocacy by clarifying how actors make strategic decisions about framing and by linking the framing process, in turn, to broader processes of norms change. Pioneers in social movement theory have identified mechanisms central to contentious politics across space and time,[32] and this book contributes to such evolving literature with the addition of blocking and backdoor mechanisms.

Methodology and Plan of the Book

The case studies central to the book are representative of a wider series of campaigns that occurred during the 1990s, and they are significant on substantive grounds.[33] The Bangladesh campaign helped raise the issue of child labor to international prominence and resulted in the first-ever memorandum of understanding brokered between business, government, and United Nations agencies to assist child workers removed from factories. The Mexico campaign involved the first and only gender-focused complaint lodged against a government by activists using the labor side accord to the North American Free Trade Agreement (NAFTA). Each case has generated considerable debate over how to prioritize rights and over the impact of such choices on the lives of people these campaigns were intended to help. Each has also generated a considerable output of scholarly and popular analysis that has influenced subsequent policymaking.

In selecting two cases in the post–Cold War era, the aim was to rule out explanations for norms evolution that centered solely on the Cold War divide, a factor already extensively discussed in the literature on human rights. Bangladesh and Mexico, though both developing countries, are vastly distinct in terms of level of development, culture, colonial history, and so on. Yet the two campaigns analyzed both focus on rights abuse in export-oriented manufacturing settings. The cases were selected for their policy relevance, and the mechanisms were inductively derived as part of a larger endeavor at theory building.

The empirical data for the book were collected through over one hundred interviews with people involved in or affected by the two campaigns. In both case studies, representatives of at least six of seven sectors (i.e., business, union, NGO, government, multilateral institutions, academia, and workers) were interviewed either in individual or focus-group settings, using standardized questionnaires. (The interview questions are available in appendixes 1 and 2.) The research aims were to gauge how participants and other actors in key sectors understood human rights issues; to identify their normative benchmarks; to interpret why and how those understandings evolved (if at all) over the course of a given campaign; and to identify corresponding actions taken by actors involved in the campaigns (or influenced by them) as a result of changes in normative understandings.

Primary source documents served as an additional empirical resource for the book. These included campaign posters, flyers, communiqués, reports, documents posted electronically to the websites of numerous NGOs and networks, along with official documents produced by the governments of the United States, Mexico, and Bangladesh. Secondary source materials were also a source of empirical data; these included reports compiled by academics and by representatives of bilateral, regional, and multilateral development organizations and private business associations and related journalistic accounts.

Process tracing[34] was the principal method of inquiry, employed to tease out the mechanisms at work in each case (i.e., blocking and backdoor moves). Moving between microlevel analysis of framing and macrolevel analysis of norms evolution, this book analyzes how the two episodes of transnational advocacy relate to a broader process of human rights norms evolution in the 1990s.

The following chapter further elaborates on the methodology and discusses the two mechanisms identified in the book, along with their operational specification. The chapter then presents a typology for how campaigns emerge and explains how several specific processes and conditions influence campaign evolution. It traces the conceptual evolution of labor and economic rights in a number of literatures and positions the book theoretically in relation to contemporary debates.

The third chapter explores a campaign to prevent the employment of children in Bangladesh's export garment industry. Thematically, the case centers on the struggle over interpreting the "best interests" of working children. Institutionally, it explores how the high-profile threat of bilateral trade sanctions ultimately resulted in a first-of-its-kind memorandum of understanding between business, governments, and UN organizations covering child welfare and factory monitoring. Procedurally, the case illustrates how actors "blocked" a campaign's dominant human rights message until it was revised to accommodate their priorities.

Chapter 4 explores a transnational campaign to prevent pregnancy screening of women employed in Mexico's *maquiladoras* (export-oriented manufacturing sites along the U.S.-Mexico border) and a national campaign to prevent the practice in other sectors more generally. Thematically, the case centers on gender discrimination as a trade and human rights issue. Institutionally, it explores how activists used the labor side accord to the North American Free Trade Agreement (NAFTA) to make the first gender-based complaint introduced under the side accord. (The NAFTA side accords on labor and environment are themselves "firsts"— the first such agreements and corresponding institutions to be created in contemporary trade law.) Procedurally, the case illustrates how activists used "backdoor" moves in an attempt to change the frame of a human rights campaign.

The fifth chapter analyzes "lessons learned" from the Bangladesh and Mexico cases. It assesses their impact on concrete policy outcomes, human rights theory, and popular organizing strategies, almost ten years after the end of the campaigns' active phases. This chapter moves beyond the narrow time frame of the campaigns themselves (sketched out in chapters 3 and 4) and links them to broader analysis of a decade of labor and economic rights protests in the 1990s. The final chapter summarizes the book's theoretical contribution and empirical findings and explores the applications of the concepts developed here to other policy settings.

2

Conflict and Change within Advocacy Networks

Theoretical Underpinnings

Human rights norms—though some of the best-codified and most socially salient norms—were the focus of considerable debate in the 1990s. During this period the process of naming human rights violators and "shaming" them into redressing wrongs changed, as activists made labor and economic rights grievances the focal point of a wide range of advocacy efforts.

The images from this period are iconic. Teenaged Central American factory workers, testifying on Capitol Hill about labor rights abuses in the factories where they worked producing clothing for U.S. consumers. A small Pakistani boy—once a carpet weaver chained to a loom—accepting a global human rights award before cheering crowds. Protesters clad in "turtle" costumes, linking arms with burly trade unionists in the streets outside the 1999 Seattle meetings of the World Trade Organization, demanding that environmental and labor standards be made part of global trade rules.

Prior to the 1990s, most international human rights campaigns centered on civil or political rights abuses such as egregious violations of personal, physical integrity (torture, disappearance, and so on). In the 1990s, however, the breadth of human rights claim making widened. Why?

Norms entrepreneurs (i.e., altruistically motivated individuals who "promote norms or ideas because they believe" in them)[1] have traditionally played a leading role in transnational human rights advocacy, launching campaigns in defense of others. They were certainly involved in bringing Central American teenagers to testify before Congress, for example. But this book focuses on the comparatively underexplored role of activists on the "receiving end" of such campaigns—actors, for example, who live in the developing countries targeted by campaigns and who may challenge the initial normative frames advanced by the "senders" in an effort to advance alternative understandings of human rights.

Receiving-end activists often have fewer material or political resources than do the senders, and this book highlights the significant finding that "receivers" nevertheless have alternative means of influencing the evolution of normative understandings central to the campaign—specifically, by employing blocking and/or backdoor moves. It also highlights the multiple drives—altruistic as well as material—that motivate actors involved in transnational advocacy. The book explains why and how normative understandings evolve as a result of interactions between senders and receivers. And it explores how changes in the way norms are understood affect agenda setting and action on the ground in the context of transnational advocacy.

The process by which norms emerge and evolve is not a straightforward one. Much of the related scholarly literature has delved so deeply into the historical specificity of particular norms that it has been difficult to generalize about broader patterns and mechanisms. Or it has tended to assert the "given" quality of norms and their social construction without explaining how these givens come to exist, or how social construction takes place.[2] Recent scholarship on the "life cycle" of norms by scholars such as Martha Finnemore and Kathryn Sikkink,[3] however, includes an innovative theory of norms evolution divided into three stages: emergence, tipping point and related cascade, then finally internalization.

This book offers new mechanisms to help interpret what happens *beneath* these three streamlined stages. It focuses on the first stage—norms emergence—and offers a novel explanation for how normative understandings emerge and evolve in the context of transnational advocacy. Contestation over different definitions of human rights norms (driven by blocking and backdoor moves) happens during the first phase in the norms "life cycle." The life cycle itself is the macrolevel context within which microlevel mechanisms (i.e., blocking and backdoor moves) emerge, as actors on the "sending" and "receiving" ends of campaigns seek to promote distinct understandings of human rights.

Clifford Bob has also explored intranetwork tensions in the context of transnational advocacy, and the ideas in this book dovetail with his and extend them in new ways. Bob analyzes the interplay between three key groups of actors involved in norms emergence: (1) local groups that seek to transform their grievances into rights claims; (2) international human rights NGOs and intellectuals that act as "gatekeepers," screening such claims and deciding which to transmit to the international level; and (3) states and international organizations that translate claims into rights in a procedural sense, codifying and institutionalizing them. He highlights the underexplored phenomenon of "countermovements"[4] that arise in response to new claim making. Using examples such as the right-to-life movement, Bob demonstrates that there may be opposition to new rights claims (such as sexual or reproductive rights) and that such opposition may be mobilized from among groups in civil society.

Bob then outlines a three-stage process through which new rights emerge: (1) the shift from grievance to claim; (2) placement of a proposed right on the agenda of international NGOs, i.e., "gatekeepers" (which, he argues, is an underexamined stage); and (3) the state-decision phase. He argues that the decisions made by gatekeepers to either accept or reject new claims as rights "often hinge on the match between a new norm or rights claim and an NGO's substantive, cultural, tactical, and organizational characteristics. If a proposed new right does not 'fit,' it may be rejected" by the gatekeeper(s), Bob argues.[5]

As demonstrated in this book, however, gatekeeper NGOs are not the only ones to accept or reject claims based on assessments of issue "fit" and/or organizational capabilities; so do groups on the receiving end of campaigns (including local NGOs themselves), which go through a similar evaluative exercise in responding to the normative claims put forward in the context of international campaigns. Countercampaigns (countermobilization, in Bob's terminology) may involve blocking or backdoor moves, made by local groups in response to international activism that does not "fit" with local human rights understandings or priorities.

Bob's work on countermobilization implies that groups involved therein tend to be less progressive than advocates of new rights.[6] By contrast, this book does not characterize countermobilization as a primarily regressive force in norms evolution—but rather, simply as a force distinct from mainstream human rights activism. Whether groups involved in countermobilization put forward more or less progressive interpretations of rights is an open question; arguably, the two cases discussed in this book involve countermobilization in which receiving-end activists sought more expansive definitions of key human rights (i.e., more progressive ones) than did senders.

This book highlights normative contestation within Bob's second stage—in the interaction between local NGOs and gatekeepers—but my focus is not on how gatekeepers interact with groups proposing new rights, but rather on how local activists respond to international campaigns once launched. The local activists who responded to the two campaigns analyzed in this book were very much interested in promoting human rights—but their emphasis was on a different, or fuller, interpretation of those rights than the one put forward by advocates on the "sending end" of the campaigns. The countermovement on the receiving end is not necessarily regressive, simply different. Where this book and Bob's work converge is in recognizing that different normative understandings *within networks* can have a significant impact both on norms evolution and on policy outcomes: "Different norms and norm interpretations compete with one another. The relative power of competing movements and counter-movements will play a major role in determining the norms adopted by states, and more importantly, how those norms are implemented in fact. In the end, norms will represent an amalgam of interpretations and approaches, both domestic and international."[7]

Organized around a comparative study of framing processes in the context of transnational advocacy campaigns or protests, this book thus focuses on framing—the naming of wrongs and claiming of rights[8]—because it is a process integral to setting the normative agenda of a campaign. The cases analyzed in the succeeding chapters demonstrate that a mix of normative and material interests influence how activists choose their normative reference points; how they negotiate with the actors targeted by the campaign (such as business or government leaders); how activists negotiate *with one another* over the evolution of a campaign's frame; and how they take action in the arena of contentious politics. Blocking and backdoor moves are central to this complex process of norms evolution.

Identifying when blocking or backdoor moves take place is challenging because it involves a "double hermeneutic" (i.e., interpretation by a scholar of the interpretations of actors). To avoid imputing particular normative understandings to actors who do not hold such understandings,[9] the book assesses how specific normative reference points—such as the human rights treaty language invoked by activists—change over the course of a campaign. It draws upon a range of sources (primary and secondary), including in-depth interview data, to tease out the progression of norms evolution in each case.

Placing "New" Rights in Context

The dichotomy between civil and political rights, on the one hand, and economic, social, and cultural rights on the other marked government policymaking for much of the latter twentieth century. Although the 1948 Universal Declaration of Human Rights (UDHR) includes a comprehensive list of rights, separation between the various types prevailed in the two major UN conventions on human rights drafted subsequently: the International Covenant on Civil and Political Rights, and the International Covenant on Economic, Social and Cultural Rights. Proponents of keeping the two conventions separate argued that civil and political rights are "enforceable, or justiciable, or of an 'absolute' character," whereas economic, social, and cultural rights can be implemented only "progressively," subject to the economic constraints of states. The former, it was argued, should be "immediately applicable"— they are "rights of the individual against the State"—while the latter can be achieved only over time.[10] This separation has marked succeeding scholarship on rights, with its emphasis on "generations" of human rights (first, second, and third).

Though nonbinding, the UDHR was the inspiration for scores of constitutions throughout Africa, South and Southeast Asia, and the Caribbean, adopted after these countries reached independence in significant numbers in the 1960s and 1970s. These postcolonial constitutions—many of which were drafted following socialist-inspired independence struggles—created entitlements in a more explicit manner than did many Western constitutions (though this is a matter of degree on both sides).

Among Western constitutions there is variety as well. European social welfare democracies generally have constitutions informed by a social democratic view of economic rights. The state bears a much heavier social development burden than it does in the United States, for example. Whereas European policymakers tend to view labor and economic policy issues as rights based, those in the United States tend to view labor rights issues as limited to preventing the most egregious types of work-related personal injury—and tend to view economic policy as wholly separate, a matter of fiscal policy choice, not of rights. Economic development is not a right, it is the byproduct of market-led growth, U.S. policymakers have typically argued. Development assistance is not a right; it is the result of government or private largesse. The European Court of Human Rights has thus made considerably more progress than either U.S. courts or the Inter-American Court system in interpreting law on economic rights.[11]

Latin American law oddly straddles the fence on human rights questions. Like European law, it tends to emphasize the social welfare responsibilities of the state (i.e., responsibilities for promoting economic rights). But social welfare ministries in Latin America typically operate not as rights-based institutions but as entities charged with meting out benefits from the state on a highly discretionary basis. Similarly, labor-monitoring bodies throughout the region are prone to inefficiency, budgetary constraints, patronage, and lack of interplay with other human rights institutions. Decades of authoritarianism ended with a region-wide shift toward democratization in the late 1980s and early 1990s, and with it came a blossoming of human rights mechanisms (state and non-state) focused on civil and political rights protection and promotion. But these bodies remain largely separate from institutions charged with protecting labor and economic rights.

The dominant human rights paradigm for the past century, worldwide, has thus been civil and political rights as human rights. Not until the late 1990s was it challenged, when anti-corporate-globalization activists, among others, began to frame their grievances and demands in terms of human rights. A pitched battle over whether or not to attach labor standards to trade agreements raged in the 1990s, with the United States government pushing for linkage (largely in response to American labor) while business leaders and neoliberal economists within the United States itself balked at the linkage. Many developing country governments also resisted labor standards linkage, on the grounds of sovereignty and alternative cultural values.[12]

Long the champions of the "right to development" within the United Nations system, official representatives of these same countries have tended to be strongly in favor of increased development assistance but wary of formally linking trade and labor standards, lest they compromise the comparative advantage many developing countries enjoy based on low-wage labor. The authoritarian leaders who have governed many developing states have insisted internationally on the primacy of economic and social rights over civil and political ones—even after the eclipse of the Soviet Union, the fall of socialism, and the rise of neoliberal policy orthodoxy in the 1990s—in order not to come under the spotlight themselves for civil or political abuses. At the grassroots level, however, interesting divisions have emerged within and among developing countries over the degree to which trade and labor standards should be linked.

Finnemore and Sikkink have thus rightly observed that "new norms never enter a normative vacuum but instead emerge in a highly contested normative space where they must compete with other norms and

perceptions of interest."[13] Sorting out the basic normative understandings at stake and mapping change over time are essential to interpreting
whether and how activists' own human rights understandings have
evolved from beginning to end of these campaigns, and whether or not
these changes have led to the emergence of broader patterns of rights
discourse beyond the campaigns themselves.

Activists involved in the 1990s campaigns on labor and economic
rights linked competing definitions of rights to distinctly corresponding
remedies; through contentious politics, they demanded concrete remedies from the entities they targeted (both state and corporate actors). In
the process, they opened a wider debate over how human rights would
be understood, protected, and promoted in a post–Cold War, highly
globalized era.

This book takes the rhetorical battles over labor and economic rights
seriously. They are more than smokescreens for struggles over resources.
They are also processes through which actors renegotiate the meaning
and content of social practices—in this case, how rights should be protected and promoted. Negotiating understandings within a campaign is
only part of the struggle; activists must also persuade actors that hold
power to respond to a campaign's demands. Framing the rights and
wrongs at stake is a critical step in the process of negotiating solutions. It
is the step this book focuses upon centrally.

Norm evolution is not automatic. It is highly contingent on a range of
factors discussed later in this chapter, including the manner in which a
campaign is launched, whether or not sanctions are threatened, and
whether or not the various individuals and groups on both "ends" of a
campaign share interests. The blocking and backdoor mechanisms identified in the Bangladesh and Mexico cases are central to understanding
how the process of norms evolution unfolds in the context of transnational advocacy.

Both mechanisms have the potential to change the dominant message
of any given human rights campaign as a whole. Blocking resulted in a
significantly broadened transnational frame in the Bangladesh campaign, whereas backdoor moves resulted in only minor alterations to the
campaign frame (and those only at the local level) in the Mexico case. A
goal of the book is to set the stage for broader theorizing on the conditions under which blocking and backdoor moves succeed or fail in alter-
ing campaign frames over a wider range of cases.

Clarifying Key Terms

Though the UDHR presents an interdependent and indivisible vision of human rights, labor rights and economic rights developed on two distinct paths—and on a different track entirely from mainstream human rights advocacy—at least until the 1990s.[14] *Labor rights* are commonly understood as rights of people in the workplace. They entail an employer-employee relationship. They imply a fixed physical work setting. They include fair wages, working hours, protection against forced or abusive labor, freedom of association and collective bargaining, nondiscrimination, and equal access to work. Labor rights have both negative- and positive-rights dimensions; they include both protections from harm and entitlement to benefits and services, for example.

Economic rights have a broader and more contested definition. Nearly half of the articles in the Universal Declaration of Human Rights are economic in nature. They include property rights (article 17); the right to social security (article 22); the right to work[15] and a living wage[16] (article 23); the right to an adequate standard of living and security in case of unemployment (article 25); and the right to education (article 26). But economic rights as human rights are not as well developed conceptually as civil and political rights, or as well measured.[17] And core human rights institutions have not addressed the protection or promotion of such rights as effectively as they have addressed civil and political ones.[18]

The terms labor and economic rights are used in this book for several reasons: First, activists themselves invoke both terms and often make distinctions between them. Some activists make claims with a narrow focus on workplace-specific grievances. Others develop protest agendas around broader economic justice claims. Often, activists use workplace-specific grievances as an entry point into broader discussions of general economic justice issues. Occasionally, activists transcend the workplace entirely and make systemic arguments about the nature of the global economic system.

Second, existing institutions and policy discourse mirror these distinctions. Some institutions, such as the International Labour Organization (ILO) or labor unions, are charged with protecting and promoting labor rights issues explicitly.[19] Others, like the World Bank, are charged with stimulating broader economic development—a necessary but not sufficient condition for ensuring economic rights, which also require the protection of equality of treatment and access. (Notably, the Bank and other international financial institutions have traditionally stressed the apolitical nature of their mandates and have avoided "rights talk.")

The split among different types of rights is also mirrored in professional circles. Labor lawyers litigate on labor law. Economists make recommendations on economic policy. International or civil rights lawyers handle the bulk of human rights litigation, traditionally defined. Only a few straddle the divides. Domestic policy structures in many countries tend to mirror these divisions. And so has public consciousness about human rights for many years. Yet participants in contemporary advocacy campaigns have challenged the distinctions among different types of rights.

This book routinely employs the term *campaign*—one widely used in literature on transnational advocacy—to imply a beginning, middle, and end to contentious action.[20] As revealed in the case studies, there is often considerable debate over when a campaign begins, the stages through which it evolves, and when (if at all) it ends. Nevertheless, the case studies are bounded temporally in an effort to map the periods of greatest intensity in transnational action. In addition, the book analyzes the entities targeted in each case and develops a corresponding narrative that clearly illustrates the relationships between context, actors, target(s), and shifts (if any) in normative discourse. As Sidney Tarrow explains, by clarifying "what people are resisting against," it becomes easier "to specify within these broad processes the *concrete mechanisms* [such as blocking and backdoor moves] that link the sources of contention to their actors, their form of contention, and their outcomes" (emphasis added).[21]

Mechanisms: An Operational Perspective

The issues analyzed in this book—norms evolution, transnational advocacy campaigns, framing—are central to a dynamic academic literature[22] and are related to some of the most compelling questions on the public policy agenda. People are concerned about the human side of global economic expansion and have begun to challenge its ethical underpinnings—often invoking the term "rights" in connection with questions of economic development.[23] This book offers the building blocks necessary to advance theory building on economic rights and norms evolution—beginning with an analysis of mechanisms. James Mahoney lists at least twenty-four definitions for "mechanism" in one review essay,[24] but in general mechanisms are a tool for explaining the *how* behind given observed phenomena.[25] They are useful in building partial explanations.[26]

Doug McAdam, Sidney Tarrow, and Charles Tilly distinguish between cognitive, relational, and environmental mechanisms—the first of which involve "alter[ing] individual and collective perceptions," as do the blocking and backdoor mechanisms identified in this book. Blocking and backdoor moves also have a relational quality, which McAdam, Tarrow, and Tilly define as the ability to "alter connections among people" by introducing new intermediaries who bring new ideas to the fore.[27] These authors admit, however, that they have left the hardest job—that of operationalizing mechanisms—largely unfinished, noting that their most recent collaborative work gives "little attention to the problems of observation, measurement and formal comparison" of mechanisms.[28] This book begins to address that challenge.

Blocking and backdoor moves differ by degree. Distinguishing between them entails comparing how the declarations and actions of people on the sending end of a campaign differ from those of actors on the receiving end. An alternative normative benchmark proposed by the receivers provides an alternative standard by which to measure rights. Judging whether blocking or backdoor moves are under way is thus a matter of degree.

A useful analogy is to think of both mechanisms as being measured on a Richter scale. Blocking is like a major earthquake: it entails overt rejection of dominant norms, and the statements associated with it are often harsh and denunciatory. So are the rebuttals. Backdoor moves, by contrast, are like tremors; they are barely evident. A person could be sitting on a fault line and not even know it, attributing the rumbling he or she feels to a passing truck rather than to an impending earthquake.

In order to identify backdoor moves, it is critical to examine any given statement or activity that takes place in the context of transnational advocacy for double meanings and intentions. For example, a training session or rally held in conjunction with a campaign may be executed not really in order to defend the dominant standard of human rights central to that campaign's frame. Rather, the event may in fact be aimed at creating a venue within which to put forth a secondary set of norms.

Recognizing blocking or backdoor moves thus requires an observer to measure the human rights claims at issue in a campaign against a separate, third standard and then to compare the rival claims against one another, using that third standard as the basis for comparison. To do so involves:

1. *Assessing what the campaign initially proclaimed as its normative base line.* How does it "measure up" to other standards that stipulate rights as well as corresponding entitlements and/or duties of various parties?

2. *Assessing how this initial baseline differs* from what other actors (such as those targeted, or potential allies, or beneficiaries) propose as the definition of human rights as well as corresponding entitlements and duties.

Do the rights claims of any party shift over time? If so how? (For example, are different actions prohibited, required, promoted or encouraged at the outset of the campaign versus mid-way through it?)

Codified norms are the most straightforward type of norm to use as a "third" standard for comparison. They range from existing official human rights treaties, declarations, and other hard and/or soft treaty law to corporate codes of conduct and voluntary corporate compliance standards. If sending activists propose one set of human rights claims, based on a particular codified baseline, and receiving-end activists respond by invoking a significantly different baseline, then blocking is likely taking place. If, however, the claims are distinct but less dramatically so, then backdoor moves are likely in play.

Actors who block a campaign message may then refer to alternative norms that are largely aspirational statements. The conventions that actors who block refer to as a baseline for their preferred, alternative understanding of human rights norms may be codified but not implemented (let alone taken for granted, or widely socially recognized).[29] Staking out aspirational human rights claims (versus making claims based on well-codified and institutionalized ones) may be an opening strategy—a stance from which activists will narrow their claims over time.

Actors who use backdoor strategies, by contrast, may decide that open opposition to a campaign's frame is not likely to be as successful as indirect influence. Or they may have normative goals closer to those proposed by the actors launching a given campaign. Operationally, the challenge for actors engaged in backdoor moves is to stake claims that, when measured against a "third" benchmark, are not as divergent as those proposed in a blocking scenario.

A range of factors influence the decision to block or make backdoor moves, which in turn influences the evolution of normative understandings within a campaign. These factors include how a campaign emerges; whether material sanctions are involved in a campaign; and whether there are shared interests between senders and receivers.

How a Campaign Emerges

Campaigns emerge in several different ways. Keck and Sikkink's "boomerang" pattern focuses on actors who seek to *change their own situ-*

ation at home (i.e., in country A) by leveraging the influence of outsiders on state or corporate actors in country A.[30] The impetus for this type of campaign thus comes from within country A itself: actors are in some way oppressed and seek change, with the assistance of outsiders. In this scenario, activists in country A enlist their allies in countries B and C in a jointly executed campaign aimed at pressuring public- or private-sector actors in country A to take specific actions. They leverage not only the influence of popular sector actors in countries B and C but also state pressure from B and C on A. Keck and Sikkink offer numerous examples of this type of campaign, in which actors have sought to protect domestic civil and political rights by enlisting international allies.

This book introduces two alternative forms of campaign emergence, distinct from the boomerang mechanism—namely, the "outside-in" and "dual-target" forms. Activists in country A may launch "outside-in" campaigns aimed at *changing conditions in other countries*—for example, country B. They target key actors (i.e., state or corporate) in country B and then build alliances with actors in countries A, B, and C to pressure their target(s) in country B for change.

The impetus for the "outside-in" type of campaign is complex: actors in country A may feel compelled by ethical or religious obligations to address the needs of the poor or oppressed in other countries, for example. Hence, they may launch campaigns to address them. Or actors in country A may have a material interest in changing the situation in country B. (They may be unionists, for example, whose rank-and-file membership insists on "getting tough" with country B over labor standards not so much for moral reasons as for material ones—i.e., to dent country B's low-wage comparative advantage, for example, and thus lessen competition.) The Bangladesh case is an example of such an "outside-in" type of campaign.

A second new type of campaign emergence identified in this book is the dually targeted campaign: activists in country A launch this type of campaign, focusing on actors both at home (i.e., within country A) and abroad (in country B, for example) and pressing for change in both arenas simultaneously. The impetus for this type of campaign may come from shared interests—such as trade treaties that bind states to mutual standards of behavior. Actors in country A thus collaborate with actors in country B to influence how standards are interpreted and implemented in both countries. The Mexico case is an example of this type of strategy.

Analysis of the boomerang mechanism has explained how allies persuade one another to participate in transnational advocacy campaigns largely in normative terms; Bob's recent work adds a critical material dimension. The present book adds another dimension to discussion of norms emergence—specifically, the distinction between "outside-in" and "dual-target" campaigns. If activists on the sending end of a campaign appear insensitive to the prevailing norms in a targeted country (their own or others), those they are seeking to influence may not be receptive to the "outside-in" introduction of a new normative understanding and may block it. And dual-target campaigns require activists on the sending and receiving ends of campaigns to share interests. These shared interests may occur by default or may have to be cultivated intentionally by parties on either end of the campaign.

Influence of Material Sanctions

Consumer boycotts were a tool that activists frequently employed in the context of cross-border campaigns for labor and economic rights in the 1990s and earlier.[31] This book analyzes the influence of such boycotts on the emergence of blocking and backdoor moves—and, by extension, norms evolution. The academic literature on economic sanctions, of which consumer boycotts are a subset, focuses principally on state-to-state sanctions (i.e., sanctions designed by states to influence the behavior of other states and/or targeted actors within such states).[32] Analysis of commodity sanctions is included in this literature, but consumer boycotts are typically referenced only tangentially.[33]

This book explores the proposition that material sanctions (in the form of consumer boycotts) threatened by outside actors in conjunction with a transnational campaign can increase the likelihood of blocking on the receiving end. Activists launching consumer boycotts often tie the threat of sanctions to the willingness of a target state or corporation to enforce labor rights. Local activists on the receiving end of such campaigns (i.e., in the targeted country) may seek to block the campaign if they believe the actions demanded by those boycotting are either unfair, impossible to achieve, or out of step with local normative understandings. Particularly when local activists feel their ability to influence the target is extremely limited, they may block in an effort to try to head off sanctions entirely, by stalling the campaign itself.

In the absence of sanctions, however, groups on the receiving end of a campaign are not faced with an immediate threat and the corresponding need to defend themselves from harm. Receiving-end activists are thus in a better position to evaluate whether they may, in fact, benefit from allowing the campaign to proceed—at least on the surface—without threatening to quash it entirely or openly challenging its normative core. In this scenario, backdoor moves are more likely to occur.

In the case studied in this book, sanctions play a role distinct from the one they have played in other prominent international human rights struggles. Whereas South Africans fighting apartheid encouraged their international allies to wage a sanctions-based transnational campaign against the Afrikaner regime from the 1970s until that country's transition to democracy nearly two decades later, the Bangladeshis blocked—actively opposing the trade sanctions threatened by U.S.-based activists involved in an American-led transnational campaign against child labor in Bangladesh's garment industry.

By contrast, direct sanctions were not a threat in the Mexico case. The drafters of the North American Free Trade Agreement had made sanctions a "last resort" for settling disputes under the NAFTA side agreement on labor.[34] Nor did Human Rights Watch (HRW)—the lead NGO in the transnational campaign launched to protest the practice of pregnancy screening in Mexico's *maquiladoras*—resort to the threat of sanctions in its advocacy efforts in this case. The closest Human Rights Watch came to doing so was to publish in its 1996 and 1998 reports copies of letters the organization had sent to high-profile corporations alleged to have carried out pregnancy screening in the *maquiladoras*. Even then, HRW did not call directly upon readers of the reports to boycott these corporations. And local activists in Mexico, though they held different normative understandings of human rights than did their U.S. counterparts, nevertheless used backdoor moves in an effort to shape the frame of this particular transnational campaign rather than employ sanctions of any type.

Influence of Shared Interests

Blocking is less likely when activists on the sending end of a campaign have at least some shared interests with those on the receiving end. There is always the possibility that activists on the receiving end may "agree" on norms only superficially and may then try to present alternative understandings through the back door. Activists often opt for such backdoor strategies when there is mutual interest in having the campaign succeed—both on the part of those launching the campaign and on the part of those responding to it. Respondents thus act to avoid signs of obvious normative discord in the interest of maximizing the likelihood of a "win-win" outcome.

Mutual interests may be normatively based or materially based. Again, Clifford Bob has pioneered in identifying the role that material interests play in transnational advocacy.[35] For example, funding, media attention, and intra- or intergroup rivalries are all relevant to consider.

Factors of this type influence how NGOs and networks decide to frame human rights in the campaigns they launch. They constrain or empower groups differently and set up a process of calculation that evolves in tandem with changes in the factors themselves. As funding levels change, as media attention waxes or wanes, as rivalries emerge, intensify, or dissipate, groups involved in campaigns will shift their human rights messages. These factors often function in tandem with one another. Well-resourced groups can afford to "buy" or attract more media attention, for example. They may also inspire greater resentment and, hence, rivalry on the part of other groups.

Because the organizations that launch campaigns are often nonprofit entities, they must be responsive to donor preferences if they are to continue receiving operating funds. Their message must connect to the policy priorities of international donors. Southern NGOs speak wearily about the "flavor-of-the-month" tendency among northern donors. Certain themes, countries, or populations fall in and out of "fashion" as multilateral, bilateral, and private donors vie to come up with new and creative policy priorities for giving. NGOs, networks, and individuals competing for scarce donor funds are forced to compete against one another for the same limited pool of funding. Discerning a donor's human rights preferences and shaping programs to match them are one strategy for fundraising.

Media attention is a second critical factor that affects the definition of interests in a transnational advocacy campaign. The sheer fact that the victims are often far away makes it important to create sharp "images" of them (video, audio, photographic) in order to convince the viewing (or listening) public to take part in a campaign—or at least support its aims politically or financially. There is a close connection between a campaign's success in doing so and its ability to raise funds more generally.

Intragroup rivalry is a third factor that helps shape interests and is often closely related to the struggle both for funding and for media exposure. Members of the tightly knit networks of people involved in international campaigns can ostracize as effectively as they can include one another. Longstanding political differences, personality clashes, betrayals, and dashed expectations are just as much a part of transnational advocacy as international brotherhood and sisterhood.

In the Mexico case included in this book, for example, the decision to frame rights in terms of feminist discourse or labor struggle depended as much on how women perceived the feminists "at the helm" of that movement in Mexico as it did on deep-seated beliefs about feminism per se. It was also colored by longstanding rivalries between groups based along the U.S.-Mexico border and their counterparts in Mexico City.

These center-periphery tensions are widely analyzed in political science literature and take on new meaning in the study of transnational labor and economic rights advocacy.

Concluding Observations

In all three types of campaigns (i.e., boomerang, outside-in, and dual-target), actors on the sending end of a campaign make strategic decisions about how broadly or narrowly to define human rights issues. They develop an initial rights "frame" based not only on their core beliefs but also on how they think actors on the receiving end will perceive the message and respond. Sending-end activists determine who their allies are and what issues will resonate with the media, donors, and the public at large. They develop strategies for framing human rights on multiple levels, taking all these factors into consideration.

Actors on the receiving end engage in the same process of multilevel analysis in deciding how to respond to a campaign. They may embrace the definition of human rights central to the campaign's main message and decide to take part in the campaign. Or they may oppose the definition, the message, and with it, the campaign itself. Their strategic decisions about accepting the human rights frame presented—or blocking it, or presenting alternatives (overtly or subtly)—are influenced by the factors discussed above, including the manner in which a campaign emerges, the presence or absence of sanctions, and the degree of shared interests. In the process, receiving-end activists also determine who their allies are and how issues will resonate with the media, donors, and the public.

Activists themselves do the heavy lifting of framing. They "generate collective action frames which dignify claims, connect them to others, and help produce a collective identity among claimants."[36] But they do not act alone. Their opponents as well as potential allies—along with "elements of the state, third parties, and the media"—all play a role in framing.[37] Though the tendency in scholarship on contentious politics had been to characterize framing as an activity carried out solely by activists at the opening of a campaign, more recent work has highlighted the interplay of a range of actors and the ever-evolving nature of frames themselves. This book maps changes in the way human rights are framed over the course of two campaigns, taking into consideration a wide range of actors involved in the process while focusing principally on the role of sending- and receiving-end activists.

The case studies in the chapters that follow extend and develop the theoretical discussion laid out in this chapter. They show that norms emergence is a complex, often counterintuitive, and fascinating process—one in which norms entrepreneurs themselves often play a supporting (not a starring) role, and in which the norms that ultimately emerge as a campaign's main "message" are often quite distinct from those voiced at the outset. The Mexico and Bangladesh campaigns demonstrate the central role of blocking and backdoor moves in this evolutionary process.

3

Child Labor, Child Rights, and Transnational Advocacy

The Case of Bangladesh

In the early 1990s child labor in Bangladesh's garment export industry spurred international controversy. United States legislators threatened formal trade sanctions against the country, and thousands of American consumers pledged to boycott garments made there. Bangladeshi activists, in turn, responded by blocking the very campaign ostensibly aimed at helping child workers in the garment industry. Why? How did the actions of activists on the receiving end of this campaign ultimately affect the way children's rights[1] were framed in the campaign and beyond?

This chapter explains the process by which activists in Bangladesh blocked the central human rights message of this transnational campaign until the campaign's human rights frame (and corresponding policy priorities) evolved to reflect a broader interpretation of children's rights than solely the right to be protected *from* child labor. Local activists blocked the dominant frame of the anti-child-labor campaign until it broadened to include children's right *to* education and basic income.

As a result, the definition of children's rights employed by activists and policymakers in the United States (i.e., on the sending end of this transnational campaign) evolved: from a narrow, civil- and political-rights-based definition of child labor as protection from harm, to a broader definition that included children's economic rights to education and basic income.

The campaign began with the introduction of the Harkin bill on child labor (1993); continued through the launching of a consumer boycott organized by the U.S.-based Child Labor Coalition (1995); and ended with the 1995 signing of a memorandum of understanding between business, government, and United Nations agencies that brokered a three-year set of policy initiatives on child labor in the garment industry. The chapter contextualizes the campaign by explaining its antecedents, active phase, and aftermath. Throughout the case narrative, key factors that influenced the decision to block are introduced and analyzed—and their generalizability and implications for comparative analysis beyond the case are also explored.

Campaign Antecedents

In the late 1980s, several major news organizations focused on international child labor—including the Cox newspapers, the *Washington Post*, and the *Christian Science Monitor*. All ran extended series focusing on child labor, which several members of the U.S. Congress cited directly while introducing related legislation in 1987 aimed at banning imports into the United States of products made with child labor.[2]

The normative benchmarks for child labor at this time were limited—indeed, children's rights as a human rights issue were in an emergent phase. Staff directly involved in drafting the anti-child-labor legislation noted the absence of an "easy definition" of "internationally recognized child rights." The UN Convention on the Rights of the Child had not yet been drafted (it would not be until 1989), so congressional staff opted instead to use ILO Convention 138 on Minimum Age (of 1973) as their normative reference point. This convention lays out minimum-age guidelines for countries at differing levels of development. Legislators focused on controlling the problem in the export industry alone—"the area that elicits the most consensus and elicits the most moral outrage"—arguing that "much of the world has accepted the proposition that children under the age of 14 ought not be working in industry and in factories."[3]

Over the next two years (1989–91), anti-child-labor legislation continued to wend its way through Congress.[4] A growing American citizens' lobby against child labor gained visibility as well. The Capitol Hill Forum on the Exploitation of Children in the Workplace (November 1989) fostered dialogue between legislators and many of the NGOs, church groups, and consumer and human rights organizations that would later unite to form the Child Labor Coalition (CLC).

In Bangladesh itself, a battle was shaping up over how to determine the "best interests" of working children and how to define human rights in relation to those interests. Rosaline Costa, a former Bangladeshi nun, championed the child labor issue in these early years, building alliances with American activists and their supporters in the U.S. Congress and other sectors of American government. Costa was a norms entrepreneur whose intent was to spotlight child labor in the garment industry in Bangladesh and to shame government and local businesses into reform: "I began to think, 'Why should the children sell their blood so cheaply, while others are making money out of them?' I started this campaign by my own self when I saw that children (as young as seven or eight years old) worked in this factory from 8:00 a.m. till 11:00 or 11:30 p.m. I felt it was inhuman to use them like this."[5]

Costa sought the help of outsiders who could bring pressure to bear on her government and on companies manufacturing in the sector because she deemed it "impossible to do anything in Bangladesh."[6] Although outsiders had focused attention on child labor generally in the late 1980s, Costa was instrumental in focusing their attention specifically on Bangladesh. She made two visits to the United States in 1990: the first hosted by the U.S. Information Agency and the second by the AFL-CIO-affiliated Asian American Free Labor Institute (AAFLI). These labor organizations would become instrumental partners in Costa's struggles back home.

Between Costa's first and second trips to the United States, the AFL-CIO filed a "worker rights petition on Bangladesh" with the Office of the United States Trade Representative (in June 1990), seeking to condition continued trade assistance under the GATT's General System of Preferences (GSP) on improvement of working conditions in Bangladesh. Centrally referenced were problems of child labor in the Bangladeshi garment industry. The AFL-CIO's petition was rejected in 1991, but the union was not deterred from resubmitting petitions in 1999 and 2000.[7]

Costa followed the strategy of many other international human rights activists, seeking to shame her own government and business sector into recognizing abuse of working children by invoking outside pressure—in this case, the pressure of American unions. She also sought to galvanize the U.S. government and American consumers into recognizing their complicity in consuming goods made with child labor. Viewed in this manner, the case appears a classic example of "boomerang" advocacy.

Yet while Costa nurtured valuable union and NGO alliances in the United States, she was unable to win many Bangladeshi activists over to her cause. And here, the Bangladesh case departs from the standard script of boomerang advocacy campaigns. Costa remained largely isolated: she was considered a social pariah—harassed by government security forces for bringing "shame" to her own country, dismissed by other local activists, allied much more strongly with outside NGOs than with those at home. The role of local NGOs who opposed Costa's actions became more significant than her own in determining how child rights/human rights issues were framed by this campaign. Their blocking would ultimately play a stronger role than her persuasion in shaping the outcome of how children's rights norms evolved in this case.

The Bangladesh case thus offers an example of "outside-in" campaign evolution: Costa's inability to enlist significant domestic support meant that there was not a local base sufficient to marshal a boomerang-style campaign (in which receiving-end activists would have been more likely to welcome the outside actions taken in their favor). Instead, the anti-child-labor campaign was launched largely from "outside" Bangladesh and was perceived locally as both out of sync with local normative understandings and as contradictory to local interests—thus increasing the propensity of local actors to block.

Phase I: The Harkin Bill

By spring of 1991, members of the U.S.-based United Food and Commercial Workers' Union (UFCW) had launched "Mothers' Day" demonstrations at stores of the American retailer Wal-Mart to protest the use of child labor in Bangladesh, urging: "Attention American Mothers! . . . Because it is impossible to determine whether any item has been manufactured by child labor, the only way for Americans to stop Bangladesh factories from exploiting child labor is to stop buying all clothes made in Bangladesh until that country ends child labor."[8]

The UFCW union's 1991 Mother's Day boycott principally challenged Wal-Mart's use of "Made in USA" labels on clothing subcontracted from factories in Bangladesh. It was, in a sense, a warm-up act for a more far-reaching consumer boycott that would come in the wake of legislation introduced by Senator Tom Harkin of Iowa in August 1992. Following the lead of colleagues in Congress such as Representatives Donald Pease and George Miller, Harkin introduced his version of the Child Labor Deterrence Act—or "Harkin bill," as it became known (S. 3133)—aimed at eliminating child labor in export industries worldwide.[9] The Harkin bill threatened U.S. government trade sanctions on any industry producing goods with child labor.

An evening documentary produced for *Dateline NBC* in December 1992 focused explicitly on child labor in Bangladesh; footage of Bangladeshi children sewing garments for Wal-Mart was central to the program. Thereafter, citizen outcry over child labor in Bangladesh's export garment industry reached a crescendo. In March of 1993, Senator Harkin reintroduced his bill (S.613), which he argued was aimed at "eliminating a major form of child abuse in our world. . . . *This legislation is not about imposing our standards on the developing world. It's about preventing those manufacturers in the developing world who exploit child labor from imposing their standards on the United States.* . . . [C]ountries do not have to wait until poverty is eradicated or they are fully developed before eliminating the economic exploitation of children. In fact, the path to development [is] to eliminate child labor and increase expenditures on children such as primary education" (emphasis added).[10]

Never in any of its iterations did the Harkin bill specifically reference Bangladesh as a target. But policymakers, business leaders, activists, and others interested in the garment industry in Bangladesh deemed the country a likely first target for trade sanctions were the bill to become law. Harkin specifically referenced evidence of child labor in the Saraka Garment factory of Bangladesh, given to him by "a former Catholic sister" (i.e., Rosaline Costa) who had visited the factory in November 1992: "She said that 60% of the 500 workers in the factory were boys and girls under the age of 13."[11] The senator's effort to stress that the 1993 bill was "not about imposing our standards" emerged in response to the heated opposition his bill had already begun to generate within Bangladesh itself.

Manufacturers in Bangladesh began massive layoffs of children employed in the garment industry shortly after the Harkin bill was first introduced in 1992. Garment industry lobbyists in Washington, DC, had warned manufacturers in Bangladesh of the coming storm,[12] and the layoffs began thereafter. Although initially denying publicly the presence of child labor, members of the Bangladesh Garment Manufacturers and Exporters Association (BGMEA)—the principal industry association for the garment industry—were quick to rid themselves of children in their factories.[13]

Local Bangladeshi papers warned in December 1992 (at the time of the *Dateline NBC* documentary) that were the Harkin bill to become law and Bangladeshi garment exports to be sanctioned by the United States, "cautious estimates say some 40,000 to 50,000 low age workers would be driven out of the garment industry . . . fuelling serious social problems in urban areas."[14] The threat of sanctions was thus a second factor that predisposed activists on the receiving end of the anti-child-labor campaign to block, given the potentially crippling effect sanctions would have had on the local economy.

According to ILO estimates, child laborers in Bangladesh number some 1.9 million below the age of ten and make up 12 percent of the country's total workforce of 51 million. The U.S. Department of Labor estimates that 19 percent (6.6 million) of children between the ages of five and fourteen work; of these, 5.4 million are between the ages of ten and fourteen. The garment sector employs but a "tiny fraction" of that overall number (i.e., less than 10 percent).[15] Nevertheless, the publicity surrounding the 1992 *Dateline* episode and the Harkin bill was impossible to ignore: were the bill to have been implemented as law, Bangladesh would likely have been an opening target. The mere threat of sanctions alarmed companies in the garment sector—and, by extension, the government and public of Bangladesh.

The textile industry is Bangladesh's largest manufacturing sector and generates fully half of all industrial employment.[16] The "ready-made garment" subsector (RMG) generated 74 percent of the country's $5 billion in exports in 1999, employing some 1.5 million people in manufacturing.[17] Of these, between 80 percent and 95 percent are women; fully 70 percent of all female employment in the formal manufacturing sector takes place in the RMG industry.[18] Over the past four decades, the industry has grown "almost without any assistance from the government."[19] It has expanded from "only a few units" in 1977, to 21 factories in 1982, to some 50 factories in 1983, to upward of 2,400 by 1997, to almost 3,000 factories by 1999.[20]

At the time of the Harkin bill and the subsequent consumer boycott launched by the Child Labor Coalition in 1995, the United States imported some $901 million worth[21] of garments from Bangladesh—nearly half of all Bangladesh's exports.[22] A threat to a sector this vital to employment and export earnings was understandably considered a threat to the national economic security of Bangladesh.

Phase 2: Blocking Begins

As soon as word of the Harkin bill circulated in summer 1992, a wide range of commentators in Bangladesh and beyond were quick to denounce it and to warn of its potentially damaging effects. Articles in the local press ranged from relatively moderate critiques of what such commentators deemed a naïve effort out of sync with local development realities, to vitriolic attacks that cast the Harkin bill as part of a larger, neocolonial plot to keep Bangladesh underdeveloped and weak. Among the fiercest responses was that of commentator Farhad Mazhar, who argued that the Harkin bill was simply an "attempt to maintain business interests with the excuse of 'human rights.' . . . [T]he imperialist process has put on the garb of 'human rights,'" he charged.[23]

Less stridently, the Dhaka-based paper *The Daily Star* editorialized: "[T]he gauge [the United States] applies for maintaining the standard often proves greater than our society, in the absence of so many supporting conditions and factors, can agreeably respond to." Anticipating the American argument that children should be in school, not at work, the author continued: "Child workers earn . . . at least to feed themselves or to supplement their parents' income; and in worst cases, to solely support their families. If they could not get employment in the garments factory, chances were that either they had to put their labour into more hazardous or harder jobs or simply had to sit idle. But the prospect of their going to school surely would have been nil. So laws do not speak to the whole story."[24] A supporting argument typically ran: "It's like forcing the poorer countries, where a minimum social safety net is absent, to *swallow the Western standard of human rights*" (emphasis added).[25]

The normative references for the early versions of the Harkin bill were the 1959 UN Declaration on the Rights of the Child and 1973 ILO Convention 138 on Minimum Age—neither of which included provisions on child empowerment central to the later 1989 UN Convention on the Rights of the Child. This meant that the opening position of American activists who used the Harkin bill as a centerpiece of their "outside-in" campaign was similar to Costa's normative position—but far from that of other activists in Bangladesh who may have acknowledged the normative undesirability of child labor but who argued for its necessity on economic grounds.

Local activists in Bangladesh were quick to point to the country's poverty as the underlying reason for child labor and to fault the Harkin bill for worsening the condition of child workers like one whose mother explained, "I had no choice [about sending my son to work], it was not possible for me to run my family on my income. My job is very unreliable. I have to feed all of my children."[26] An August 1993 editorial in the Bangla-language daily *Janakantha* echoed this sentiment more generally: "It is true that the use of child labor cannot be accepted. It is an inhuman practice. *On principle, we are against child labor. But the reality is different*. . . . [C]hild labor cannot be stopped completely without attaining self-sufficiency in socioeconomic fields" (emphasis added).[27] Similarly, editors of the local daily *Dainik Bangla* argued: "We also believe that children must not be allowed to work in the factories, but *no matter how humane the UN and the ILO conventions are, we do not believe that these documents would agree to a situation where children are likely to go hungry*. We think that the US should consider the social reality of the Third World before adopting the Harkin Bill. . . . *We also want children to get justice if they are compelled to work. It is a question whether depriving them of work will be justice to them.* Third World nations hope that the US will realize this" (emphasis added).[28]

Local NGO activists helped shape the ensuing public debate in Bangladesh—strategically capitalizing on the public debates surrounding the Harkin bill to reiterate key themes, while in many cases crafting alternative policy proposals to accompany their distinct view of children's human rights. The prominent human rights organization Ain-O-Salish Kendra was one such group. Nur Khan Liton, a member of the group, argued in a September 1993 article in the *Dhaka Courier* that Senator Harkin had misinterpreted the legal standards he invoked as justifying a complete ban on child labor. Light work by children, she argued, was not only permitted under ILO Convention 138 (on minimum age) but in some cases was absolutely necessary:

> In calling for the elimination of child labour, Sen. Harkin has drawn attention to ILO Convention No. 138, Article 2. But it should be noted that Article 7 concedes that in special conditions of underdevelopment, children between the ages of 12–14 may be permitted to perform light work, as long as they can avail themselves of schooling opportunities. Sen. Harkin has totally ignored this realistic recommendation in the Convention. . . . [W]e feel that *Sen. Harkin's rash recommendation is likely to affect children's right to basic necessities rather than lead to education.* The reality of child labor in developing countries needs to be understood. (Emphasis added)[29]

Though acknowledging that child labor is not intrinsically desirable, Liton argued that eliminating it without providing for remediation and education programs would not be in the best interest of poor children. She thus sought to block the campaign by proposing an alternative normative benchmark—the UN Convention on the Rights of the Child—and corresponding policy remedies focused on children's right to development:

> It is a clear violation of the terms of the [UN] *Convention on the Rights of the Child* to force these children to work and deprive them of educational or recreational opportunities. . . . Long before Sen. Harkin's bill was placed in the US Senate, trade unions and activists in Bangladesh had been struggling for an end to child labour and for the implementation of ILO conventions, and national labour laws. . . . The children working in various industries in Bangladesh, whether in garments or in other sec-

tors, live in relatively better circumstances than their neighbors in *bastis* [slums] or in villages. . . . *The right to food is no less important than the right to liberty. Freedom from hunger is no less important than civil and political freedoms.* . . . We have to recognize the reality of our situation before we can devise effective ways to change. (Emphasis added)

Liton—like other activists as well as members of Bangladeshi business and government circles—voiced skepticism that Harkin's motivations or those of the American activists involved in the anti-child-labor campaign were purely humanitarian. She called for greater fairness in the global economy as the ultimate solution to the problem of child labor: "[B]ehind the humanist demand for protection of child rights lie the demands of a protectionist economy. . . . [The solution] will require a restructuring of the international economy so that underdeveloped countries are not vulnerable to economic pressures (such as structural adjustment policies) from multilateral agencies."

The threat of sanctions ratcheted up the pressure on Bangladesh daily, and the level of local opposition to the Harkin Bill mounted apace. The U.S. Embassy in Dhaka hosted a press conference in August 1993 aimed at responding. American labor lawyer and activist Terry Collingsworth, the regional representative of the Asian American Free Labor Association (AAFLI)—the organization that had assisted Rosaline Costa in the early stages of her efforts against child labor—was the main speaker. Collingsworth reiterated that the Harkin bill was not solely aimed at Bangladesh but applied to industries throughout the world: "[I]t *is based not on U.S. moralizing but [on] already-existing national and international regulations*" (emphasis added), an embassy cable reported to Washington.[30]

Collingsworth also sought to "debunk the notion that any textile jobs lost in Bangladesh would make their way back to the US," reiterating "his hope that industry and NGOs will find alternatives for the children. He argued that the Harkin Bill has had a positive effect in that it has brought child labor to public attention, and has led to efforts to deal with the problem. When a journalist wanted to know what gave the US the right to enact the Harkin Bill, Collingsworth repeated that the US is just enforcing existing laws, and that Bangladesh only needs to comply if it wants to enjoy access to the U.S. market."

The U.S. press conference did little to stem local criticism, however. Within a week, Bangladeshi trade unions and women's rights NGOs held their own press conference to ramp up their criticism of the Harkin bill. Local NGOs called for a countercampaign on the part of local civil society organizations. A wire story from United Press International quoted one of the participants in the conference, Farida Akter, as saying: "No child works 10 to 12 hours a day for a paltry wage for the fun of it. The need for survival forces them to take up jobs in factories instead of going to school. . . . To throw these kids onto the streets would be a serious violation of their human rights." The report continued: "Akter said the [Harkin] bill only relates to export-oriented industries, and not to child labor itself. She said if the United States wants to protect rights of children, then initiatives should be taken against child labor as a whole, not just on exports. 'Clearly, this is protectionism in the guise of children's rights,' she argued."[31]

Separately, a U.S. Embassy cable to Washington on the same day noted that Farida Akter had *"called upon all quarters to come forward for waging [a] movement against the Harkin Bill and side by side protecting the children's rights.* She also called for enacting law regarding utilization of child labor"(emphasis added).[32] Hameeda Hossain, founder of the human rights group Ain-O-Salish Kendra, also took part in the press conference. Several years later, when explaining her organization's position, she argued: "We were opposed to the Bill for two reasons. First it did not take into account the reality that termination of children would not resolve the problem of poverty, nor end child labour, it would merely transfer child labour to other forms, and perhaps worse forms of work. Also we did not think trade controls are a democratic way of changing policy environments."[33]

In organizing their own press conference and openly calling for the establishment of a local "movement against the Harkin bill," activists on the receiving end of the transnational campaign against child labor in Bangladesh clearly blocked. Several factors influenced their decision to do so: the "outside-in" nature of a campaign out of sync with local normative understandings of human rights; and the threat of sanctions. Yet their efforts were not wholly uniform, and blocking was far from monolithic in nature and degree. As indicated by the range of commentary in the local press, there were distinctions among the perspectives of actors involved in the "blocking" process. Local Bangladeshi activists who blocked the Harkin bill campaign developed a range of alternative views on child labor.

Among the NGO activists directly involved in opposing the campaign were several involved in children's rights advocacy and development-related activities in Bangladesh. One was Suraiya Haque, founder of Phulki (an organization that provides daycare services in factories throughout Bangladesh). As she recalled: "I did oppose [the Harkin bill]. Because considering the socio-economical condition of the Bangladesh, those girls would go [into] more hazardous work. . . . In my opinion there is no child labor in garment sector (at least the big factories) but those girls have gone into a more hazardous work. Definitely not gone back to school."[34] Zina D'Costa, formerly with the NGO Shoishab (a group that promotes the rights of working children) argued along similar lines. "Bangladesh being a relatively poor country," poor children have to "support their family otherwise the family would die of starvation. And also the child laborers who lost their job due to this campaign, had to [become] sex workers, as there were no other alternatives before them. So we had to oppose the campaign. . . . Shoishab did get involved in their own capacity, working with other organisations in *lobbying against the bill*" (emphasis added).[35]

Indeed, one of the most gripping claims made by local activists and reiterated by representatives of international organizations such as the ILO and UNICEF was that children dismissed from work in the garment industry had gone into prostitution. Former ILO child rights expert Rijk van Haarlem, active in Bangladesh at that time, explained that the initial version of the Harkin bill made "no provisions for rehabilitation [of the children]. Many were faced with destitution. It is assumed that thousands of them sought and found other, often more dangerous jobs. Some ended up in prostitution."[36]

Data on the actual number of children working as prostitutes as a consequence of the Harkin bill are scarce. Yet this claim took on the air of truth and was repeated by the Bangladeshi press, policymakers, business, and NGOs—as well as by representatives of UN organizations and European NGOs. Bangladeshi activists defended their interpretation of child rights—one that included the right to work, lest children suffer worse consequences (i.e., prostitution)—by pointing to evidence of grievous bodily and moral harm to children dismissed from the garment factories. They blocked the Harkin bill campaign by using the same strategy Keck and Sikkink[37] have observed widely among international campaigners: they asserted the primacy of physical integrity as a nonderogable right. Their innovation was to tie protection of that right directly to analysis of the economic rights (and vulnerability) of child workers.

Northern activists, however, resisted such linkage. They asserted that there was little proof of the link between the Harkin bill and child prostitution. If children went into prostitution at all, it was not Senator Harkin who was to blame, they argued, but Bangladeshi employers who had failed the children from the outset. Unionist Tim Noonan,[38] activist Terry Collingsworth,[39] and former U.S. Department of Labor officials Sonia Rosen[40] and Andrew Samet all made this argument independently of one another when interviewed. As Samet argued: "[T]here was this prevailing kind of view that all these kids [who] left the garment factories became prostitutes. . . . I know there are people invested in finding that to be the case. . . . But I don't know if they've been able to. Moreover, if in fact that is so, whose fault is that—who is responsible for that? . . . It's an unfortunate event, but I don't think that somehow the U.S. government was responsible for that. That is the responsibility of the people who fired [the children], or mistreated them."[41]

Apocryphal or not, the claim that fired child workers were going into prostitution had the effect of pushing economic rights issues to the forefront of negotiations among business, the Bangladeshi and United States governments, United Nations organizations, and NGOs. Local NGOs opposed to the Harkin bill garnered support from a number of European NGOs and from the Dhaka field office of the United Nations Children's Fund (UNICEF). Together, these groups criticized the American-led campaign against child labor as being out of touch with the reality of working children.

Ruby Nobel, who was a staff member in the Bangladesh office of the NGO Save the Children–Sweden at the time of the campaign, recalled that "most" of the organizations that took part in the Harkin bill campaign "were from the developed countries." Among those from Bangladesh that took part, she observed,

> [s]ome . . . were doing [so] to meet their vested interests—they grabbed this opportunity and sought funds to start a programme/campaign against working children with little or no clear concept on the issue. And of course, there were no dearth of donors to feed those "greedy" organizations. [We thus] characterized it as a campaign about vested interests . . . it was just concerned about kids in the garment sector but not working children in general. . . . We have been involved in the campaign for children's rights and specially their *right to be heard*. And the [Harkin bill] campaign in many ways was a far cry from what we were fighting for. . . . We *worked closely with UNICEF to influence policy makers, civil society to address the situation with a long term perspective for the benefit of working children*. (Emphasis added)[42]

Birgitta Ling, Nobel's colleague at Save the Children–Sweden, echoed these concerns. Activists should "plan [their] interventions carefully and look at the children in a more holistic way and not only at the work they are doing," she argued years later. Ling has often cited the Harkin bill and the memorandum of understanding later brokered between business, government, and UN organizations "as examples of *how the Western world should not behave if they want to make life better for working children in developing countries*" (emphasis added).[43]

Phase 3: The Child Labor Coalition Boycott

By late 1994, members of local Bangladeshi NGOs, alarmed by the growing numbers and dire situation of displaced child garment workers, assisted a small group of them (some fifty-three children) in "ask[ing] for help in their deteriorated situation."[44] There is little to no published information on who helped the children frame their grievances. Rosaline Costa claims that a local Bangladeshi union assisted the displaced children in presenting their grievances and that AAFLI, in turn, advised the local union on how to help the children.[45] Terry Collingsworth was at that time AAFLI's regional representative and a member of the Child Labor Coalition.

In September 1994, Senator Tom Harkin officially released the first in what would become a six-volume series of annual reports on child labor and related issues, produced by the U.S. Department of Labor under the title *By the Sweat and Toil of Children*.[46] The related press release from Harkin's office noted that the Harkin bill itself "funds programs on child labor prevention, and the protection and rehabilitation of child workers, in an effort to address the *underlying causes of child labor, such as poverty, poor education, and lack of opportunity to attend school*" (emphasis added).[47] As different versions were drafted and introduced, Harkin's bill evolved over the course of the next several years to include economic rights protections more explicitly.[48]

The Child Labor Coalition, too, moved to accept the receiving-end activists' demand to include economic rights explicitly in the bargaining framework. Blocking thus appeared to have had its desired affect: Senator Harkin and the Child Labor Coalition had to make explicit their support for economic rights. Given horrific claims of child prostitution, the Child Labor Coalition insisted that the garment manufacturers themselves must assume responsibility for the welfare of children displaced from the factories. Central to any agreement negotiated among the parties, the CLC urged, should be both a remediation program and a factory-monitoring program.

Pharis Harvey, co-chairman of the CLC, had long argued for linkage between trade and human rights standards.[49] The group now made these concerns central to its lobbying with the American and Bangladeshi governments as well as with the Bangladesh Garment Manufacturers and Exporters Association. Blocking pushed the American activists to broaden the way they framed child rights—to include economic rights issues explicitly.

At the time the Harkin bill was reintroduced in 1993, Pharis Harvey had challenged: "[W]e want Congress to examine other policies of the

United States, whether in foreign aid or in lending by multilateral institutions. It will be of no use to bar the products of child labor if the US is at the same time fostering it indirectly through policies that encourage cheap-wage exports without labor standards protection or that put the burden of debt relief on the backs of the poorest people in developing countries."[50] Harvey's statement signaled an open acknowledgment of economic rights on the part of American NGOs at the helm of the campaign.

Why, then, did the Child Labor Coalition make the subsequent decision to proceed with a consumer boycott—one of the most widely criticized aspects of its overall involvement in Bangladesh? Representatives of the CLC and their supporters have steadfastly argued that they made this move as a last resort. From 1992 when the child labor issue first hit the headlines till 1995, most members of the Bangladesh Garment Manufacturers and Exporters Association (BGMEA) balked not only at having to educate or otherwise rehabilitate displaced child workers but also at allowing transparent monitoring of members' factories. The association essentially stalled the progress of negotiations for over a year (1994–95), despite the CLC's hope that a draft memorandum of understanding under negotiation would be signed during a visit by then First Lady Hillary Clinton to Bangladesh, scheduled for 31 March 1995.[51]

By spring 1995 it appeared that the association was no closer to signing the proposed agreement than it had been a year earlier. The number of children who had by then been fired from factories without provisions for their well-being had swelled into the tens of thousands. On 19 April 1995, representatives of the coalition warned BGMEA that a boycott would officially begin within one month, on 20 May 1995.[52] Following the association's rejection of the proposed agreement, the coalition solicited approval from its membership for a boycott.[53] Pharis Harvey wrote to the president of BGMEA, explaining the rationale for the boycott as follows:

> BGMEA's decision to terminate the children without contributing towards their rehabilitation falls far short of the minimum standards of social responsibility that the Child Labor Coalition has required and the [draft] Memorandum of Understanding contained. . . . On Monday, May 22, we will announce this boycott to the press, to major garment importers, and to all our constituent member organizations. . . . The American people . . . will certainly refrain from purchasing Bangladeshi garments. . . . We were prepared, if you had signed the MOU, to begin a campaign to tell consumers to "Buy a Blouse from Bangladesh and Send

a Kid to School," encouraging consumers to give *preference* to BGMEA garments as the products of a model industry. . . . However, your rejection of the MOU has made that impossible."[54]

The change in tactics on the part of the coalition is significant: as long as the Harkin bill appeared stalled in Congress (i.e., unlikely to become law) and negotiations over the agreement dragged on, members of the BGMEA could afford to deny the accusations of the campaign and could resist taking concrete action. When it appeared that consumers would move an industry boycott forward regardless of whether the Harkin bill became law or not, the industry had to sit up and take notice.

The BGMEA's swift response several days later was to launch a counteroffensive against the Child Labor Coalition. The leadership of the CLC, worried about the impact on children of a continued standoff, responded formally in a letter from Pharis Harvey to the BGMEA president. Harvey urged negotiations on the agreement and offered to "suspend the next phase of the campaign. . . . [W]e will not suspend the boycott itself but we will postpone for one week from today the next, mass phase of our work." The coalition also offered to "communicate our position to importers and retailers in this country [i.e., the United States], and to ask for their cooperation with a plan for humane, phased elimination of child labor in Bangladesh." Harvey insisted that "success [for the industry] must not be on the basis of the exploitation of children."[55]

Child Labor Coalition staff and members have long argued that their main interest was the well-being of working children in Bangladesh. When blocking on the part of local Bangladeshi NGOs made it apparent that the American activists' message needed to broaden in order to incorporate children's economic rights explicitly, they did so. Moreover, when it became apparent that sustaining the boycott would deepen the children's suffering, the CLC called it off. As Darlene Adkins, national coordinator of the coalition, explained, the coalition was "very immediate in responding" to the industry association's threat. "We ended the boycott almost as soon as it began—it was very short-lived mainly because it was more of a tactic than anything."[56] The CLC took the additional step on 2 June 1995 of writing thirty major American manufacturers, reporting that a memorandum of understanding was "being drafted for approval" at a meeting the following day (Saturday, 3 June 1995) and requesting companies to "respond to this situation—both to support this model program, as well as to help end the US consumer boycott of Bangladesh garments."[57]

Negotiations in Dhaka gained steam thereafter—with the U.S. and

Bangladeshi governments now centrally involved, and BGMEA moving toward a compromise on the language, funding, and monitoring provisions of the memorandum of understanding. By 29 June 1995, Adkins wrote to the CLC membership requesting that they take "urgent action" to halt the boycott by 5 July 1995 and send letters endorsing the memorandum of understanding to American Embassy staff in Dhaka, to be read at the signing (planned for 4 July): "This is extremely important, as we wish to show both BGMEA and its members, as well as the international press, that the *boycott was driven by our concern for children—not a plot by US groups to destroy the Bangladesh garment industry as was oft repeated in the international press*. . . . The [Child Labor Coalition]-launched boycott was valuable in bringing the parties back to the table to renegotiate. We should be pleased with our efforts which helped achieve what will probably prove to be an historic agreement" (emphasis added).[58]

American ambassador to Bangladesh David Merrill had engaged personally in high-level intermediation among the various parties from 1994 through 1995, and it was he who brokered the final agreement.[59] The U.S. Department of Labor followed the negotiations closely and rallied other international donors to support remediation and education efforts. The department also marshaled support for the agreement in the U.S. Congress.

Senior Department of Labor official Andrew Samet requested that Senator Harkin be prepared to formally endorse the agreement and explained that "the survey and implementation oversight is being left to UNICEF, the ILO and the Embassy. This may raise some skepticism with other NGO groups. . . . but the agreement itself is a very important precedent." In the description of the agreement, Samet noted that it "helps Bangladesh enforce its existing national laws on factory labor under age 14. *No new definitions of age are being introduced from abroad*. . . . UNICEF is also mounting larger programs for many other Bangladeshi children who are in the informal sector and are not covered by this MOU" (emphasis added).[60]

Samet's comments were aimed at rebutting criticism that the memorandum of understanding was an outside/Western imposition of foreign values that ignored child labor beyond the export industry. By insisting that the age standards were not a foreign imposition, Samet sought to persuade critics that the solution to the child labor problem drew on local understandings of children's role in society—and that these Bangladeshi labor laws and work standards themselves stipulated that people under the age of fourteen should not do factory work. His efforts to ensure normative buy-in on the part of opponents to the agreement signaled a shift on the part of the U.S. government that paralleled Senator Harkin's and the Child Labor Coalition's own shifts toward a more public embrace of economic rights issues.

Under the terms of the three-year memorandum of understanding signed on 4 July 1995, the Bangladesh Garment Manufacturers and Exporters Association pledged $900,000 for stipends/schooling over three years. UNICEF pledged $175,000 for alternative schools in the first year, with additional funds thereafter. The ILO pledged $250,000 for a survey of displaced children, as well as for monitoring and stipends in the first year, with additional funds thereafter.[61] Stipends for children were set at 300 taka per month—roughly one-third of what many child workers would earn in a month.[62]

Children's salaries in Bangladesh vary widely, depending on the kind of work they do and their gender, and at the time of the MOU, garment factory jobs tended to pay more than other work and were highly sought after. The stipends granted under the MOU were roughly equivalent to $6.50/month (at an exchange rate of 46 taka to 1 $US dollar). Working children could earn anywhere from the equivalent of $6 per month to $23 per month, depending upon the occupation. Typically, boys work 7.7 hours per day and are paid an average 4.6 taka per hour (i.e., 17 cents per hour, or $1.30 per day). Girls work 9.0 hours per day and are paid less— an average 2.7 taka per hour (i.e., about 6 cents per hour, or 54 cents per day).[63]

Aware that the proposed stipends might not go far enough to replace income lost by working children taken out of the factories, the drafters of the memorandum of understanding envisioned giving the children's work to family members and setting up family credit programs later. But for children faced with the immediate loss of a significant source of income and only the promise of income replacement programs down the line, the option of schooling would become less attractive over time.

After the Boycott

Following the 4 July signing of the memorandum of understanding, the Child Labor Coalition officially called off its boycott the next day.[64] As part of the terms of agreement of the MOU, the International Labour Organization conducted a survey from August to November 1995 in which it identified roughly 10,000 children in two thousand factories who were removed from work and became eligible for schooling/ stipends.[65] The percentage of workers who were children in BGMEA factories dropped thereafter from 43 percent to 3 percent over the next six years (1995–2001).[66] Still a matter of dispute, however, is the fate of the estimated 30,000 to 40,000 children fired *before* the agreement took effect.[67] Critics argue that the hardships faced by these children undermine any appraisal of the campaign (and resulting memorandum of understanding) as a success on other levels.

Yet blocking by Bangladeshi activists on the receiving end of the campaign had significantly influenced the manner in which American activists articulated children's rights, as well as how policymakers and business developed programs in response to the needs of working children. Darlene Adkins of the CLC points out that "we have never threatened a boycott since. . . . Our role is public education. We try to get the ball rolling and to involve key actors to solve problems. We don't have the financial resources for longer-term things. We bring key players in and [facilitate] a good-faith effort to solve problems. . . . It's not like we just stir up the water and when it's all muddy walk away. But it's not our role to craft each and every solution to every problem. All of the situations are different and complex."[68]

It is less clear what impact the campaign had on changing the views of Bangladeshi business, government, press, and civil society. At least publicly, business and government actors in Bangladesh have attempted to turn the black eye of the anti-child-labor campaign into a benefit. They argue that the garment industry learned from this chastening experience and is better for it. Abdul Hai, a garment manufacturer in Bangladesh, argued: "The MOU helped human rights. More facilities are following guidelines . . . the third-party auditors can come and check the factories and we're maintaining human rights conditions. . . . We have to compete in terms of human rights—this is the only weapon we have. . . . Because China isn't going to care about human rights. . . . [T]hey aren't helping human rights, so they shouldn't get the business."[69]

Privately, however, business leaders have expressed their concerns that the human rights issues central to the anti-child-labor campaign were far more complex than American activists realized and that the MOU's long-term impact was limited. Shabbir Ahmed, a Bangladeshi garment entrepreneur based in the United States, argued: "We are fully aware that it's an important issue. But you are talking about a country [that] is smaller than the state of Wisconsin, with a population of 130 million people."[70] From Ahmed's perspective, child labor "is more or less an issue of surviving. . . . Yes, I understand that the common man in Bangladesh knows that he has the right to survive, the right to live. But again, when he is constantly thinking about his own survival—and literally, because he does not know where his next meal is coming from—I don't frankly think that he has time to think about human rights."[71]

Mustafa Kamal, an official in Bangladesh's embassy in Washington, DC, expressed similar views. On the one hand, the campaign had the positive effect of encouraging people in Bangladesh to "start shunning child labor in the garment industry. . . . They began to feel that this is wrong—that awareness wasn't there before. Average people now want education and a good life for their children—instead of assuming that work is the only option for them." But "[t]he issue of child labor will never come from the Third World. It will come from the developed world." The real human rights lynchpin for Bangladesh, Kamal argued, is not child labor but trade access: "On the negative side, although the industry is now free of child labor, it's suffering from broader competitive pressures. Its demise would be devastating to Bangladesh economically and socially."[72]

To the extent that they focus on child labor today, most groups in Bangladeshi civil society tend to focus on the "worst forms of child labor" or on child empowerment. Their normative reference points are ILO Convention 182 on the Worst Forms of Child Labor and the UN Convention on the Rights of the Child, rather than ILO Convention 138 on Minimum Age. Nazrul Islam Khan, general secretary of the Bangladesh Institute of Labour Studies (a union-affiliated research institute), noted that the "campaign against child labour has always been a priority [for us]. . . . We have been working for the elimination of child labour in the hazardous industries, including garments industries. Currently, we are working to create *awareness against the worst forms of child labour*" (emphasis added).[73]

In October 1996, UNICEF released a study by an Indian researcher, Nilima Chawla, which argued that the memorandum of understanding "takes a holistic view of the rights of working children. This approach places the right to education and the right to protection within the perspective of other rights, such as the right to an adequate standard of living, which is often directly dependent on the child's financial contribution to the family's survival." As Chawla explained:

> The 20th century notion of childhood current in most international human rights legislation and social policy planning is based on an ideal of schoolwork, play and protection from any form of economic activity. The reality is that children in many countries have no schools to go to or cannot afford them, and must work if they are to eat. . . . Set within the framework of a child's rights perspective, this is the first time such an

> MOU has recognized the importance of safeguarding the interests and welfare of the children. It has also recognized the need for providing appropriate alternatives for education and income maintenance.[74]

The blocking that took place in the Bangladesh case thus resulted in a blending of human rights perspectives. The central normative reference point of the CLC campaign moved from ILO Convention 138 (on minimum age) to the UN Convention on the Rights of the Child, a standard both Bangladeshi and American activists could embrace. Controversy over the Harkin bill and the ensuing campaign ignited a broader discussion within the ILO and international policy circles on the nature of child labor and the optimal way to address it. This paved the way for the passage in 1999 of ILO Convention 182 on the Worst Forms of Child Labour, which clearly distinguishes between hazardous, exploitative forms of child labor and other, acceptable types of child work.

Over time, many Bangladeshis came to acknowledge that the most exploitative forms of child labor are not simply a necessary evil but can be prevented. Americans involved in the campaign began to realize that the "solution" to the problem of child labor must be a long-term one and that interventions on civil and political grounds must be balanced with economic, social, and cultural rights concerns. The memorandum of understanding drafted reflected this tenuous balance in words. ILO Convention 182 codified these shared understandings several years later. However, the challenge of translating such new understandings into action remains complex and ongoing.

Explaining the Campaign

Child labor is not a new phenomenon. The process of industrialization in many advanced economies entailed a stage in which child work was a mainstay of factory- and home-based industrial production. Agriculturally based societies throughout history have relied on children as supplemental workers on family farms. In addition, children have played a key role in informal sector work such as street peddling or unregistered forms of service activity, like domestic service work. Children continue to take part in all of these types of economic activity plus many others that are considerably more hazardous and detrimental to their development. The ILO estimates that more than 200 million children are currently working, worldwide.[75]

So why was there such an outcry over child labor in Bangladesh's garment industry? Why the concern about child labor in a sector that is relatively more protected and less exploitative than others? And what does the battle to protect the "best interests" of children in this case reveal about the broader processes through which norms evolve? Several kinds of explanations, when "nested," help shed light on why this case evolved as it did and in particular how blocking moves emerged and in turn helped transform normative discourse.[76]

Rationalist Interpretation

Protectionism is often invoked as the explanation for the campaign against child labor in Bangladesh's garment industry.[77] According to this interpretation, material interests trumped all others: the rights of children were little more than a public justification for a campaign grounded in protectionist interests on the one hand and economic nationalism on the other. Normative claims about children's rights were a scrim behind which competing economic and political interests fought their real battles.

American labor unions, beleaguered by low-wage competition from abroad, could have raised the specter of child labor in the Bangladeshi garment industry as a way of denting the competition. Although Bangladesh is one of the poorest countries in the world today,[78] by the early 1990s it was a major source of "ready-made garments" imported by the United States and a significant player in this sector globally. The American NGOs involved in the campaign were either pawns of unions, this argument runs, or principally motivated by the potential media attention and resources they stood to attain by participating in such a campaign. United States legislators who championed the issue were in turn beholden to special interests (among them, American unions) and cared more about reelection than about children's rights. And groups in Bangladesh that opposed the campaign were likely more concerned about the potential negative economic impact on the garment sector than about problems faced by working children.

Rationalist considerations indeed played a part in this story but cannot alone account for choices made on either the sending or receiving ends of this campaign. Rosaline Costa's initial decision to champion the plight of child laborers, for example, was arguably motivated as much by her moral convictions as by interest in expanding her network of contacts or funding sources. So, too, were the decisions of other actors on both the sending and receiving ends of the campaign. Other explanatory frameworks are necessary to flesh out an overall explanation of why and how this case unfolded as it did.

Structural Interpretation

The rise of post-Fordist production and with it the reorientation of the global garment industry toward highly mobile, offshore export platforms are structural factors that have influenced the way the ready-made garment industry evolved in Bangladesh.[79] So, too, the feminization of global export industries pushed women (and, in many cases, their children) to seek work in the sector. In Bangladesh, the tens of thousands of children fired from garment factories in the early 1990s were "mostly girls under the age of 14," according to UNICEF.[80]

These structural factors, in turn, shaped the type of actors in the sector, the broader gender dynamics at play, and the nature of workplace pressures and demands, along with the character of international solidarity efforts.[81] By extension, the way the campaign evolved was also affected. Efforts to determine the "best interests" of children "for" them gave way to a process in which children demanded their right to be heard (in the open letter to campaign activists, discussed above)—not unlike the process through which core concepts of women's human rights and related advocacy evolved in the 1990s.[82] Feminist activists in Bangladesh took a key role in blocking the Harkin bill campaign because of their concern over its potentially devastating impact on a sector dominated by female labor, old and young. They ensured that their voices would be heard by organizing the "counter press conference" discussed earlier in this chapter.

At the same time, the rise of neoliberal economic ideology, and with it the near eclipse in the 1990s of alternative economic paradigms, could also be invoked structurally to explain why one particular definition of human rights was ascendant over another. For much of the past half-century, civil and political rights (the safeguards of individual property rights) have received greater attention and multilateral backing than economic, social, and cultural rights—never more so than in the wake of the Cold War.[83] Not surprisingly, human rights campaigns by civil society organizations in the industrialized countries as opposed to those in the developing ones tended to mirror this split.

Yet these structural factors alone do not explain this case. Structure significantly influences the context in which action takes place, but it does not wholly foreordain or foreclose the outcomes that result from individual choices. Actors within campaigns and outside of them make decisions motivated in part by material drives and in part by normative ones. Individual agency is one of the most compelling aspects of this case. Choices about how to frame rights in campaigns such as this one are the focus of a rich literature on contentious politics and social movements. This literature, too, can help explain the case.

Social Movement Interpretation

Social movement theory offers yet more insights into why the Bangladesh campaign unfolded as it did and how human rights understandings evolved in the process. Put simply, savvy activists in Bangladesh and the United States focused on a high-profile industrial sector (garments), on an NGO sector replete with potential allies, and on an issue area (children's rights) that was salient in public discourse. They identified a political opportunity (the growth of the sector and potential American protectionist backlash), a mobilizing structure (well-developed NGO sectors in both countries), and a frame (children's rights—the definition open to interpretation) and capitalized on them to launch a skillful campaign.

In tandem with the growth of Bangladesh's garment sector, media and citizen interest in industrialized countries such as the United States was building around sweatshop issues in the 1990s. Unions, NGOs, and journalists increased the salience of these issues for manufacturers and consumers alike. The political opportunity for a campaign of this type existed. Similarly, the mobilizing structures were in place. Bangladesh has also been a laboratory for development assistance, the recipient of millions of dollars of foreign assistance since its independence in 1971, much of it channeled through the NGO sector. Bangladeshi NGOs have been remarkably innovative, pioneering in the development of microcredit and family planning strategies.[84] By the 1990s Bangladesh's own NGO sector was well organized and engaged in both domestic and international policy advocacy.

Finally, the frame was set: global discussion of children's rights had been sparked in 1989 by the adoption of the UN Convention on the Rights of the Child (CRC), by the UN World Summit for Children that followed in 1990, and by the subsequent widespread ratification of the CRC. And sweatshop issues, as mentioned above, had moved to the top of the opinion pages and prime-time slots of media outlets worldwide in the 1990s.

Social movement theory, then, offers valuable insights into why and how the Bangladesh campaign unfolded. But other analytic tools are necessary to tease out how the diversity of views central to framing can give rise to conflict, contestation, and new interpretations of norms. Mechanisms such as blocking are central to unpacking this process. As discussed, two of the major factors that influence blocking—an "outside-in" campaign and sanctions—were present in this case, increasing the likelihood that Bangladeshi activists would block the anti-child-labor campaign launched by Rosaline Costa and her U.S. allies.

In the end, the interpretation of children's rights evolved over the course of this campaign against child labor. A definition of child rights initially grounded principally in civil and political rights gave way to a broader one that included economic rights dimensions. Blocking served as a central mechanism in this process. Activists in Bangladesh blocked the dominant human rights message of the anti-child-labor campaign partly in response to an "outside-in" campaign out of sync with their normative understanding of children's rights, and partly in response to the threat of economic sanctions. The case thus yields insights into what happens on the "receiving end" of transnational advocacy and helps explain how new normative understandings emerge in the context of cross-border campaigns and beyond.

4

Discrimination, the Right to Work, and Reproductive Freedom

The Case of Mexico

Pregnant women who seek work or are employed in Mexico face a conundrum. They are not hired—or are readily fired—so that employers can avoid paying three months of maternity leave required under Mexican labor law.[1] Employers argue that administering pregnancy tests is necessary to keep women from abusing a generous social welfare system. For many women, paid work represents a lifeline of economic security for themselves and their families, so they hide their pregnancies—resulting in injury and, occasionally, miscarriage. Those who are not yet pregnant face the stark choice between maternity and paid employment.

Beginning in 1995, Human Rights Watch (HRW), a New York–based nongovernmental organization, focused on a particularly vulnerable group of pregnant workers: those employed in export manufacturing plants, known as *maquiladoras*, along Mexico's northern border with the United States. The organization worked with local Mexican groups to collect testimony from hundreds of aggrieved women. It issued hard-hitting reports critical of the Mexican and U.S. governments as well as a number of major multinational corporations. Using the labor side accord to the North American Free Trade Agreement (NAFTA), Human Rights Watch and other nongovernmental organizations submitted a formal complaint against Mexico and launched a campaign to pressure both governments to take action on the situation.

Feminists in Mexico City, in turn, launched a national-level campaign on pregnancy screening in 1998. They focused on the situation not only of pregnant women in maquiladoras along the northern border but also of those employed in government service, education, and other economic sectors throughout the country. For Mexican activists, more than the right to nondiscrimination was at stake. The right to work and society's responsibility for human reproduction were as well.

This chapter explores the evolution of these two intertwined campaigns. Rather than "block" a campaign that emphasized civil and political rights over economic and social ones, Mexican activists brought the latter rights into the Human Rights Watch campaign through the "back door" and put them front and center in their own 1998 national-level campaign. Ultimately, Mexican activists had greater influence on national policy discourse than they did on international human rights debates. Discussion in the Human Rights Watch campaign, in particular, remained publicly centered on the civil and political rights aspects of discrimination. But among Mexican activists involved in the two campaigns, economic rights, reproductive freedom, and the social construction of gender roles emerged as central frames at the local level.

Before we proceed, several additional comments on the context are necessary. Contemporary maquiladoras are manufacturing plants that "finish" production of semifinished goods for export; colloquially, they are also referred to as *maquilas*.[2] Special Mexican investment and customs rules allow maquiladoras to import machinery, equipment, and materials duty-free; up to 100 percent foreign investment is allowed. Finished products are then reexported. If a portion of the goods is sold within Mexico, import duties are paid only on the value of foreign parts—not on the total value of the finished product.[3] The number of maquiladoras has tripled since NAFTA's passage in 1994. As recently as 2001, the sector accounted for 23 percent of all Mexican export earnings—more than that generated from petroleum exports.[4]

Roughly half of all maquiladora workers are female, and many are single parents who have migrated to the border from the interior of the country and lack a network of family or community support. Although wages in the maquiladoras are low in real terms, averaging $3 to $5 per day, they are often higher than wages in domestic industry or informal sector work. Thus, women seek these jobs over others available, such as domestic service work. Prices in the "dollarized" northern border region are often higher than in many other areas of the country, and workers struggle to keep abreast of rising living costs.[5] The loss of a job for a woman alone and supporting a family, far from family and friends, can be devastating.

The Human Rights Watch campaign began in 1995 with preliminary research on pregnancy screening in Mexico's maquiladoras. It continued through the submission of a formal complaint under the procedures of the NAFTA labor side accord in 1997 and ended with the last official deliberations on the submission in 1999. The national-level campaign began in early 1998 with efforts by Mexico City–based feminist groups to shed light on pregnancy screening in multiple economic sectors and regions of the country. It continued from mid- to late 1998 with a national signature campaign, opinion survey, and tribunal. In 2000, the national-level campaign ended with the last submissions of related legislation to local and federal legislatures.

Phase I: Buildup to the Human Rights Watch 1996 Report

Human Rights Watch reports are the principal tools the organization uses to goad powerful actors that violate rights into reforming, and to spotlight failures in the international human rights regime more generally. In the mid-1990s, the organization was eager to test the efficacy of the NAFTA side accord on labor, the North American Agreement on Labor Cooperation (NAALC). Its Women's Rights Program was also keen to explore new ways of carrying out gender-based human rights advocacy. So HRW sought out allies in the NGO community along the northern border of Mexico and proceeded to launch an investigation into the practice of employment-related pregnancy screening.[6]

Human Rights Watch staff members have acknowledged that local Mexican groups did *not* propose the idea of a campaign against pregnancy discrimination. Adequate wages, housing, and safe transit to and from work are among the chief concerns most often cited by women who work in Mexico's maquiladoras. LaShawn Jefferson, director of HRW's Women's Rights Program, collected data on workers' priorities over the course of investigations for the 1996 report and the 1998 report that followed it. She was aware that pregnancy screening was not the top priority of most workers, but she knew that it fell within the mandate of the labor side accord—unlike more general economic development issues.[7]

As Widney Brown, a HRW Women's Rights Program staff member at the time, explained: "We tend to attack everything through a discrimination mode. . . . The way we're constructed as a 'women's rights' division . . . presumes a nondiscrimination model." In this case, "[o]ur decision was to take a narrow wedge issue and crack the door open."[8] Human Rights Watch thus strategically chose an issue that was straightforward to interpret in legal terms (i.e., discrimination based on gender), that fell within its mandate, and that would lend itself to adjudication under the NAALC—even if this was not the most pressing concern of activists at the grassroots level within Mexico itself. Pharis Harvey of the Washington, DC–based International Labor Rights Fund—one of the three organizations that collaborated with Human Rights Watch in filing a formal complaint against Mexico under the NAFTA labor side accord—also acknowledged that pregnancy screening was not a top priority for grassroots women in Mexico but decided to co-file the complaint because of the political saliency of the issue in the NAALC context.[9]

In some ways, then, Human Rights Watch's campaign against pregnancy screening would appear to be an example of an "outside-in" campaign—a case in which "outside" actors (i.e., U.S.-based activists from Human Rights Watch) seized upon human rights problems in another country (i.e., Mexico) and sought to remedy them from outside. But this case is more accurately a "dual-target" campaign, one in which U.S. and Mexican activists collaborated in spotlighting the complicity of both the U.S. and Mexican governments in abuse in the latter country. It was the "dual-target" nature of the campaign that will be shown to have influenced Mexican actors on the "receiving end" to make "backdoor moves" (rather than blocking ones) in this case.

A second factor that influenced the "receivers'" decision to make backdoor moves was the shared interest that both U.S. and Mexican activists had in seeing the HRW campaign succeed in shaming their respective governments. The aim was to produce a hard-hitting report that would spotlight the Mexican government's failure to prevent the pregnancy screening. Human Rights Watch intended to target companies that carried out pregnancy screening while simultaneously highlighting the U.S. government's unwillingness to pressure Mexico to enforce its own local labor law under the terms of the labor side accord. By marshaling such evidence, the organization could then submit a formal complaint under the NAALC.

In March 1995, Human Rights Watch sent a team of investigators to Mexico. Together with local activists, they collected personal testimony from hundreds of women who had suffered pregnancy-related employment discrimination. They also interviewed representatives of government institutions responsible for resolving labor disputes and monitoring factories—including state- and federal-level Conciliation and Arbitration Boards (Junta de Conciliación y Arbitraje, or JCA); the Secretariat of Labor and Social Protection (STPS, by its Spanish acronym); the Office of the Labor Rights Ombudsman (Procuraduría de la Defensa del Trabajo); and the Office of the Inspectorate of Labor (Inspección del Trabajo).[10] Researchers concentrated their efforts in cities in the states of Baja California, Tamaulipas, and Chihuahua. Separately, in late June 1996 Human Rights Watch sent letters to U.S.-based firms with manufacturing operations in the maquiladora zones of those states, demanding an end to employment-related pregnancy screening.[11]

Human Rights Watch released a report in August 1996, confirming that many companies in the maquiladora zones require pregnancy exams prior to hiring as proof that women are not pregnant.[12] Other firms require exams throughout a woman's employment; if a worker is found to be pregnant, she is moved to more physically taxing job within the factory or to a night shift, in an effort to force her to voluntarily resign for her own safety/comfort. And women are fired outright for being pregnant—though the reason for dismissal is often stated differently in official paperwork related to the firing. In addition, HRW reported that Mexico's labor dispute resolution system "is not only unresponsive [to pregnant workers' concerns] ... but also is unequipped both materially and legally to pursue such problems."[13]

As an appendix to the 1996 report, Human Rights Watch published samples of its letters to U.S.-based companies with manufacturing operations in the maquiladora zones (among them, Sanyo, Zenith, and Carlisle Plastics) along with their responses. Many of the corporations contacted by Human Rights Watch replied that the organization had written to them so late in its investigation—i.e., less than a month before the release of its report—that HRW could not have expected a reasonable reply. The bulk of corporate responses either denied or sought to justify employment-related pregnancy screening.

Human Rights Watch's report urged the government of Mexico to uphold its obligations under the Mexican Constitution, various United Nations human rights treaties, ILO conventions, and the NAALC.[14] It called upon the U.S. government to exercise political pressure on Mexico to do so and urged corporations to end pregnancy-related employment discrimination.

Backdoor Moves during Phase I

Mexican organizations along the northern border provided Human Rights Watch with invaluable assistance in producing both its 1996 report and, later, a 1998 follow-up report. Members of local Mexican groups made introductions to people in border communities. They guided HRW staff around the remote neighborhoods where maquiladora workers lived and arranged interviews with women in homes, outside factories, and in other neutral locations. They provided background information on local governmental institutions and political figures. And they distributed the finished Human Rights Watch reports to other human rights and social justice organizations in the border region.

To local nongovernmental organizations in Mexico, the campaign offered a vehicle for shaming both the United States and Mexican governments into reform, along with multinational corporations that contract from maquiladoras. Mexican NGOs had an interest in seeing the Human Rights Watch campaign succeed—even if its focus was pregnancy screening, rather than fair wages or other more pressing issues. They knew that their leverage with local (let alone national) politicians was limited and that their chances of influencing multinational corporations were slim unless they worked in partnership with other allies. Human Rights Watch was a high-profile ally, so border-based Mexican NGOs supported the organization in gathering testimony and information on the scope of the pregnancy screening problem. Mexican activists did not seek to alter the campaign's principal focus on discrimination. Instead, they brought their own longstanding concerns about economic rights and social justice into the campaign through the back door.

At the grassroots level (though not in official policy dialogue), local Mexican groups broadened the central message of the Human Rights Watch campaign. Rather than focus principally on discrimination, as Human Rights Watch did, border-based activists in Mexico acknowledged the problem of discrimination while at the same time casting the fight against pregnancy screening as part of their ongoing struggle *for* workers' economic rights and *against* an exploitative economic development model.

Members of the Comité Fronterizo de Obreras (CFO), a workers' rights network that spans several northern Mexican states, had been involved in cross-border solidarity efforts on workers' rights for decades. Hence, the CFO embedded the concern for preventing discrimination against women within its broader ongoing agenda of struggling for equitable economic development, explained executive director Julia Quiñónez: "For the 36 or 37 years that the *maquilas* have been here, we've seen increasing impoverishment. . . . This paradise, these benefits they're going to bring us—we see reality isn't changing things. It's bringing a setback in the lives of workers. . . . This is the contribution we want to make: they have to listen to what we've seen, to what's happened. That's why we're always trying to be involved in discussions about neoliberalism, so that they listen to workers."[15] Quiñónez left intact the official message of the Human Rights Watch campaign (i.e., antidiscrimination), while working at the local level simultaneously to develop an additional human rights message, focused on economic rights.

For Carmen Valadéz of Factor X (a Tijuana-based women's organization), participating in the Human Rights Watch campaign meant grafting the legitimacy of the international human rights movement onto the local struggles of working women. For her, this campaign was but an entry point into a broader human rights discussion, an opening step in a longer process:

> [L]abor rights or what happened in the *maquila* wasn't seen as a violation of human rights in Mexico. . . . When you see the news and hear about a human right you think, "Aha, the disappeared, the political prisoners, police brutality." . . . This is the first image you have about human rights. . . . *So there needs to be this link made between labor rights and human rights—with the labor rights as part of human rights. . . . Because that way, society will pay more attention.* . . . And if we don't talk about it from a gender perspective, we're never going to discover all the kinds of violations there are, nor describe them in their totality. (Emphasis added)[16]

Like Factor X, several other border-based groups that collaborated with Human Rights Watch were explicitly feminist, particularly in Tijuana—among them, Casa de La Mujer Lugar la Tía Juana and Yeuani. But intergroup rivalries over funding and political access often set these groups at odds, as did tensions over similar issues between border-based and Mexico City–based feminist organizations.[17] Most border-based groups in Mexico in fact avoided developing an explicitly feminist analysis of structural discrimination in the larger global economy that would have incorporated civil, political, *and* economic rights dimensions.[18]

Instead, groups such as CFO and Derechos Obreros y Democracia Sindical (DODS, based in Reynosa, Tamaulipas) worked from a class-based perspective.[19] Members of the Maquiladora Organizing Project (based in Agua Prieta, Sonora) resisted calling themselves feminists, despite the fact that women entirely staffed the group, which in turn served a grassroots-level population that was disproportionately female. They focused their work on social justice (inspired by liberation theology) rather than on feminism. A number of members struggled to balance their activism with "family obligations" that they felt compelled to carry out along strict gender lines. Only a few dared challenge a patriarchal division of labor within their own homes.[20]

The end result of the diversity and tensions among border-based groups, as well as their overarching pragmatism, was that nondiscrimination remained the overt theme of the transnational campaign, but

Mexican activists developed a secondary frame (i.e., economic rights) articulated locally. Border-based activists supported Human Rights Watch's antidiscrimination agenda while at the same time bringing economic rights issues in through the back door. Not until Mexico City feminists developed their own separate campaign on pregnancy screening did some groups at the border join them in raising the issue of social responsibility for human reproduction.

Phase 2: NAFTA Side Accord Complaint, Resulting Campaign, and Backdoor Moves

By May 1997, Human Rights Watch had waited eight months for either the U.S. or Mexican government to officially respond to its first report. Without a response from either, HRW began the process of filing a formal complaint using procedures established under the NAALC, jointly with the U.S.-based International Labor Rights Fund (ILRF) and the Asociación Nacional de Abogados Democráticos de México (National Democratic Lawyers Association, or ANAD). Together, the three organizations entered a formal complaint with the United States National Administration Office (US-NAO), one of the three parallel offices that exist in all three signatory countries to the NAFTA. Each office processes complaints submitted by its own citizens about labor situations in any one of the three countries; as in this case, human rights groups submit complaints jointly with counterpart organizations in the other signatory countries. At the same time that it filed "Submission 9701" (as the complaint was officially known), Human Rights Watch began the process of preparing a second report.[21] The organization initiated a second round of interviews from May through November 1997, involving NGOs and workers as well as government representatives in the cities of Tijuana, Ciudad Juárez, Río Bravo, and Reynosa.[22]

Over the course of the next six months, an intergovernmental investigation proceeded in response to Submission 9701. In November 1997, the governments of the United States and Mexico jointly hosted a public hearing in Brownsville, Texas. Representatives of the NGOs that filed the complaint offered testimony, along with women workers from Mexico.[23] In January 1998, some nine months after receiving Submission 9701, the U.S. National Administration Office responded with a recommendation for bilateral discussions between the U.S. and Mexican governments.[24]

Border-based activists in Mexico worked on a two-track strategy throughout this period. They participated actively in the official campaign organized by Human Rights Watch, giving testimony at the

Brownsville hearing, for example. At the local level, however, they continued to explain the campaign to people in grassroots communities primarily in terms of economic rights issues. For most Mexican activists in the border region, eliminating gender-based discrimination was a means to an end—that of improved economic security for women. Discrimination was indeed a rights abuse, they acknowledged, but economic injustice was an even more pressing rights concern.

Hunger, not gender discrimination, was the principal priority for poor women, argued María Santos-Ramírez of the Casa de la Mujer Lugar Tía Juana. The Human Rights Watch campaign "put forward a conceptual model of human rights and lamentably it's stayed just like that—a model. I think it's in the air and people use it, but it's not clear what it is nor how to outline it in reality. . . . In fact, it may be holding us back, because it's very floating. It's abstract. And people from below don't perceive it. And above all in the *maquila*, in a context in which women are really more submerged in their preoccupation about dinner (*la sopa*) than in this type of thing. . . . They're hungry. And they'll say, 'Well, this is important but it's just that I can't be bothered right now.' "[25] Rather than engage in a debate with staff of Human Rights Watch over the central definition of human rights that animated the campaign, Santos-Ramírez drove them around Tijuana to meet with workers, facilitating interviews in homes and outside factories. Her principal concern remained the larger problem of economic injustice in the maquiladora industry and the social vulnerability of poor women—not gender discrimination per se.

Julia Quiñónez of the Comité Fronterizo de Obreras in Piedras Negras argued similarly: "*Women's rights are important. But here the economic situation is even more important.* . . . Women ask themselves, 'How do I bring what's necessary to my household?' And this is a really serious problem—the most important, I think. When workers don't earn enough, they forget a little about themselves as they try to think, 'How am I going to better my salary?' (emphasis added).[26] As Quiñónez pointed out, the desperation for a job would lead women to hide their pregnancies; once found to be pregnant, they would lose their jobs—and be denied their right to work. For Quiñónez, discrimination itself led to a violation of another right, the right to work.

Maquiladora workers, Quiñónez argued, would often subordinate concern for civil or political rights to concern for economic ones. While acknowledging discrimination as a significant problem, she thus continued to focus her grassroots outreach principally on the right to work along with the struggle for better pay and working conditions in the industry in general. Quiñónez facilitated numerous meetings for staff of

Human Rights Watch with workers, as had Santos-Ramírez; she also participated in a number of binational events in conjunction with Submission 9701.

But at the grassroots level, Quiñónez and the members of CFO remained focused on the right to work and broader economic justice concerns. Mexican activists from the border region worked principally "through the back door" to introduce new issues into the Human Rights Watch campaign. They had little ability to influence the campaign's official agenda set by HRW, which was far better resourced and had greater political access (both in the United States and Mexico) than any of the border groups. So they opted instead for influence at the grassroots level.

Phase 3: Mexican National Campaign

By contrast, feminists at the helm of the 1998 national campaign had less need to use the backdoor moves: they had organized their own campaign and hence were able to frame their concerns independently of Human Rights Watch. While Mexico City–based feminists did echo HRW's message on nondiscrimination along with their border-based colleagues' emphasis on the right to work, they also framed their own campaign in terms of a new interpretation of the value of work and social reproduction.

Feminist groups in Mexico City embedded concern for economic rights within the national-level campaign they launched in 1998, while at the same time introducing new priorities: they sought to transform gender roles to include equal responsibility for men and women in child rearing, and to raise awareness within Mexican society of the value of "social reproduction." Rather than penalize pregnant women by taking away their employment, feminists argued, society should ensure women of comprehensive support during pregnancy, since women bear the burden of reproducing society itself.

A primer on human rights produced by the 1998 campaign summed up this argument succinctly: "If people can reconcile their work with their family, all of us will be better off because increases in quality of life are connected with increases in worker productivity. The proposal of family responsibilities is that *the care of children, the elderly and other dependent people is a social necessity* and as such, the State and private enterprises ought to cooperate in making facilities available to women and men so that they can carry out this care-giving" (emphasis added).[27]

Advancing new understandings of work, productivity, and social value would be a challenge in any setting, but particularly in Mexico, a midlevel industrialized country. Small employers, which make up the bulk of the domestic industrial sector, have argued that it is more diffi-cult for them to provide pregnant employees with maternity benefits than it is for large employers. Official agencies, such as the Secretariat of Labor and Social Protection (STPS), reflect this position as well:

> Fully 90% of the businesses in [Mexico] are micro and small-scale, and they employ 80% of the occupied labor force. . . . *For such firms, contract-ing pregnant women is an onerous burden. Business owners are the ones that carry the biggest cost burden associated with sickness and pregnancy; moreover they have to pay the person who replaces the pregnant worker.* This is the rea-son that many of them solicit pregnancy certificates [i.e., proof that women are not pregnant], and the situation has only increased with the growing participation of women in the labor market.[28]

Amelia Iruretagoyena, a professor in the border state of Sonora in-volved in the 1998 campaign, recalled participating in a meeting with representatives of the STPS as recently as fall 2001, during which "these young businesswomen expressed their discontent with the fact that other women's organizations are publicly opposing pregnancy exams. The businesswomen said that they run small businesses, and because of this, they couldn't contract people who soon would become unable to work. And to put them at ease, the organizer of the event told them, 'Look, our gripe isn't with small businesses. It's with medium and large businesses—as if to say to them, You all can take it easy. The propaganda that we're doing isn't going to affect small businesses.'"[29]

Pilar Muriedas, co-founder of a congressional watchdog group in Mexico City and a leader in the 1998 feminist campaign, reflected on the challenge of convincing the Mexican public that pregnant women play a productive role in society and economic life. The campaign "opened the debate over what it means for women's various rights to be in conflict, given the employers' perspective. And it was really important to find out what people thought," she recalled, "to find out that *they sided with the employers*, saying, 'How can anyone who's pregnant expect to be hired if the employer knows that person isn't going to produce anything?' *So we began to talk about social rights and reproduction. It's a social good, reproduc-tion—so society has to assume the costs of society's own reproduction*" (em-phasis added).[30]

Yolanda Ramírez and Melisa Villaescusa, protagonists in the national campaign, explained that the Dutch Embassy in Mexico City had awarded a one-year umbrella grant to four organizations involved in directing the 1998 campaign.[31] Ramírez herself also received an individual MacArthur Foundation Leadership Grant (as did several other activists involved in the 1998 campaign), which she used for research and advocacy on the campaign.[32] She and others persuaded allies in the public Commission of Human Rights of Mexico City to pay for flyers and a primer on basic human rights and gender that explicitly denounced pregnancy screening. Armed with these resources, the activists launched a "Campaign to Discourage Firing for Pregnancy and Pregnancy Exams."

Their aim was to capitalize on the political space created by the Human Rights Watch campaign, and the ensuing U.S.-Mexico policy dialogue, in order to push the Mexican government for a range of gender-sensitive policy reforms. As Yolanda Ramírez explained, "the theme was set. There was also the discussion of NAFTA and the parallel accords. It was a really important conjuncture, a moment when a campaign could really have impact with all this on the table. . . . *The 1997 campaign was important for what it achieved in Washington, but it was really hidden. . . . So what we did was open up the theme*" (emphasis added).[33]

Patricia Mercado, then a leader of the feminist political organization DIVERSAS (and later a candidate for the 2005 Mexican presidential election) also noted that the 1998 campaign was timed to capitalize on international attention focused on pregnancy screening: "[I]f you don't mount a campaign at the particular time in Mexico in which the public is favorable, you lose the opportunity . . . we saw an opportunity . . . because there was a year of controversy leading up to it."[34]

Mexico City feminists were reluctant to embrace the dominant normative underpinnings of the earlier Human Rights Watch campaign—which, Yolanda Ramírez argued, came from "this part [of the international human rights movement] that defends civil and political rights, but not from the movement of feminists or for women's rights. *And so we knew how to work with it to give it an additional meaning*" (emphasis added). Rather than block the Human Rights Watch campaign, Mexican feminists "worked with it," to use Ramírez's phrase, transforming the discourse on human rights over the course of their own campaign.

Ramírez and others spearheading the 1998 campaign focused on "reproductive rights of *working women*," since "women workers have always been outside the global discourse of feminism."[35] In Mexico, feminist neglect of labor concerns has been a function, in part, of the middle-class nature of the feminist movement.[36] It has also resulted from lack of technical expertise on economic issues among activists. As Eloisa Aguirre, a representative of the Women's Institute of Sonora (a government agency) acknowledged: "[C]ertainly in the area of labor, things haven't consolidated into networks. . . . I think it's because the subject matter is a little more difficult. There are not a lot of women who are in command of the material."[37] Launching the 1998 anti-pregnancy-screening campaign, then, engaged Mexican feminists in advocacy that was more explicitly economically focused, while at the same time challenging them to work with new partners (i.e., border-based groups).

Tactically, the Mexico City feminists made the blunder of not involving border-based groups in the initial planning of the 1998 campaign. This oversight ignited old center-periphery tensions, though several border-based groups eventually took an active role in the 1998 campaign. Among them, members of Factor X and Yeuani (in Tijuana), Casa de la Mujer and Mujeres en Acción Sindical (in Hermosillo), and CFO (in Piedras Negras, Reynosa, and Matamoros) helped compile signatures for the national petition circulated by the 1998 campaign. As Elsa Jiménez-Larios of Yeuani explained, "[i]t served me very well to jump into the [1998] national campaign. Because I didn't have resources for a campaign—I never did. . . . So I grabbed onto the campaign as best I could. I used the things that they did."[38]

The Mexico City feminists at the helm of the campaign pushed a multipronged agenda forward. They sought out as many avenues as possible to publicize their efforts. They circulated a national petition, denouncing pregnancy screening. They informally surveyed the public on the issue. They compiled additional individual testimony from women in sectors other than the maquiladoras and from regions other than the northern border. And they organized a national "Tribunal on Reconciling Maternity and Work," aimed at garnering high-profile political attention along with considerable media and public attention.

The tribunal, held in Mexico City on 22 October 1998, was the centerpiece of the campaign. Widely covered in the press, the event was also billed with the activists' slogan: "Human reproduction: a social responsibility," to convey the central idea that women should not be fired for being "unproductive" during pregnancy because they are contributing to society's reproduction by having children.[39]

At the tribunal, activists highlighted the campaign's central achievements: between six and seven thousand people nationwide had signed a proposal denouncing pregnancy screening.[40] The overwhelming number—78 percent of those surveyed—opposed the practice.[41] Activists shared findings from more than one hundred additional cases of pre-hire pregnancy discrimination and five cases of outright firing for pregnancy, nationwide. Women nationwide were interviewed—in Baja California, Chihuahua, Sonora, Coahuila, Tamaulipas, Campeche, Puebla, Jalisco, the state of Mexico, and Mexico City.[42] Nine women affected by pregnancy screening shared their personal testimony.[43] At the conclusion of the event, women legislators from across the ideological spectrum called upon the Mexico City legislature to support the campaign (though differing on recommendations for reform).[44]

Throughout 1999 activists involved in the national campaign continued to meet with national-level policymakers. Their efforts dovetailed with the next phase of the Human Rights Watch campaign, which was then unfolding.

Phase 4: Human Rights Watch Report 1998 and Aftermath of the Campaigns

Although the United States called for bilateral consultations on Submission 9701 in January 1998, it took nearly ten months for the talks to occur. On 21 October 1998, bilateral consultations between the U.S. and Mexican governments took place—the day prior to the national tribunal hosted by feminists in Mexico City. At the bilateral talks, the Mexican government continued to resist acknowledging that pre-hire pregnancy testing was discriminatory.[45] Human Rights Watch moved into high gear thereafter, releasing a second report in December 1998 that noted the inadequate response to Submission 9701 on the part of both the Mexican and U.S. governments.[46] The 1998 report criticized Mexico's unwillingness to recognize pre-hire pregnancy screening as discriminatory and the U.S. reluctance to challenge this position. Once again, the annex included copies of responses from various companies contacted directly by Human Rights Watch; many denied that pregnancy screening or pregnancy-related firings happened in their factories.

The United States and Mexico moved forward with plans for a joint "outreach session" on Submission 9701, to be hosted in early March 1999 at Mérida, in the state of Yucatán, Mexico. In advance of the meeting, heads of the NGOs that had filed Submission 9701 wrote to the U.S. secretary of labor, criticizing the selection of Mérida as the venue. They pointed out its inaccessibility to NGOs based on the northern border and argued that the Yucatán is a subregion with few maquiladoras and little local activism on workers' rights. Hence "the Mexican Government will be able to deny, unchallenged, its responsibility under the labor rights side agreement to NAFTA to enforce the anti-discrimination provisions of its labor law and to make labor tribunals available to those with grievances."[47]

Nevertheless, the March 1999 outreach session took place at Mérida, paralleled by a process of ministerial consultations. LaShawn Jefferson of Human Rights Watch and Julia Quiñónez of CFO broke "the monotony of the tri-national meeting" with highly publicized remarks on the problems facing women in the maquiladoras. Jefferson focused her critique on pregnancy discrimination, but Quiñónez challenged the entire premise that export-oriented manufacturing zones are the answer to poverty in Mexico. She warned that in the long run, the Yucatán would suffer the same fate as the northern border states if it were to adopt an economic development model based on lack of labor rights protection, low salaries, and social distress: "The maquilas are a mirage ... they should be the last recourse for creating jobs; they're taking advantage of our women."[48]

At this round of ministerial consultations, the government of Mexico acknowledged for the first time that pre-hire pregnancy testing is discriminatory and illegal. The United States government promised to release a report on related policy resolutions but has not done so to date.[49]

Human Rights Watch ended its campaign on Submission 9701 after mid-1999, but national-level activism on pregnancy screening continued for the rest of that year and into the following. In May 1999, the National Union of Educational Workers (SNTE, by its Spanish acronym) of Mexico negotiated an agreement with the country's secretary of education to prohibit the practice of requiring teachers to present pregnancy certificates.[50] In September 1999 Mexico City's then mayor, Rosario Robles (Partido Revolucionario Democrático), signed into force a law that criminalized the practice of employment-related pregnancy screening within the Federal District two days after she took office.[51] Legislators across the political spectrum picked up on gender themes and introduced a range of legislative initiatives in the national Congress—often goaded by the same NGOs that had taken part in the 1998 campaign.[52]

Yet workers, activists, and government and business representatives interviewed for this book throughout the border region and in Mexico City revealed deep-seated skepticism about the long-term impact of either the 1997 or 1998 campaign. Some asserted that the practice of pregnancy screening continues, albeit more occluded. Others argued that women at the grassroots level were little affected by these relatively high-profile policy exercises and remain unaware of their own rights. Still others argued that there could have been more effective ways to address the root causes of poverty and discrimination than campaigns.

Human Rights Watch, for one, published a third report in April 2001 that critiqued the entire NAALC submission process on both procedural and substantive grounds.[53] The report included discussion of Submission 9701 to illustrate that the time invested in filing and following complaints through the NAFTA side accord process had borne few concrete results for the groups involved.

From the perspective of some of the local activists involved in the Human Rights Watch campaign, there were indeed costs to following the cumbersome NAFTA-related process. Mexican activists involved in the campaign on Submission 9701 criticized the overall lack of impact it had on the lives of people at the grassroots level. Human Rights Watch had tested the side accord mechanism by launching the pregnancy screening campaign—and found it wanting. But Human Rights Watch had not developed a strategy for continued grassroots dissemination of the campaign's finding. And this—as much as the shortcomings of the NAFTA side accord complaint process—troubled NGO activists within Mexico.

As Elsa Jiménez-Larios of Tijuana argued, Human Rights Watch had neither a "follow-up strategy" nor a focus on grassroots-level dissemination and implementation. "With all the authority and power that Human Rights Watch had, we could have focused more on the impact of the work that we were doing locally, if there had been this linkage. But they didn't make it. They came, they put out the publication, they returned, they put out another and what happened to the people? So they de-linked the local groups. . . . The information didn't get to the women."[54]

Julia Quiñónez of the Comité Fronterizo de Obreras agreed that there was "a lot of publicity—but no follow-up," on the part of Human Rights Watch or the United States or Mexican governments, "despite all the de-nunciations." Companies had simply found more covert ways to test for pregnancy: "When there are denunciations or mobilizations, they tone it down a little—they lower the rhythm, they do it in a more subtle manner. But the practice continues."[55] Her colleague, Antanacio Martínez, concurred: "In their moment, these campaigns help, but afterwards they're forgotten. This is something really important: there isn't intense and constant follow-up."[56]

As Marcia Contreras-López, an activist in Hermosillo, noted, people at the local level often participate in surveys or are interviewed for studies, only to have researchers or activists fail to share results of their efforts. "Increasingly, people at the grassroots level cynically ask NGO representatives, 'Why should we bother to participate in international campaigns, et cetera? The people involved never tell us what happened.'"[57] The only way around the problem, Contreras-López argued, is for activists to link their policy agenda explicitly to grassroots advocacy strategies. Then transnational campaigns can serve as a "trampoline" that propels marginalized people into the political process. In a few individual cases, this happened in the campaigns discussed in this chapter.

For example, Teresa Hernández, a maquiladora worker in Matamoros, gave testimony at both the 1997 Brownsville hearings convened in conjunction with Submission 9701 and at the 1998 Mexico City tribunal organized by Mexican activists themselves. Reflecting on the process, she argued: "What we did during those years helped a lot. . . . [T]his tribunal in Mexico City had an impact, because they sanctioned what people in Reynosa were doing. . . . So it's important that they do more campaigns, have these events in other cities, and little by little things will change."[58] Other activists echoed Hernández's faith in the promise of progress over time. Several likened their efforts in both the Human Rights Watch campaign and the national campaign to "putting little grains of sand on a pile that will someday make a mountain."[59]

Analyzing the Normative Framework

Human Rights Watch laid out the grounds for its efforts against pregnancy screening in its 1996 report: "In many instances women find themselves in the untenable position of *choosing between their jobs and their rights*. Such employment practices constitute discrimination on the basis of sex, an invasion of a woman's privacy, and, in some instances, an undue limit on a woman's ability to decide freely and responsibly on the number and spacing of her children" (emphasis added).[60]

The distinction between a woman's *job and her rights* was central to how this campaign was framed. For Human Rights Watch, the right to employment was not on the table. Mexican NGOs, by contrast, deemed pregnancy screening a "double violation of rights: on the one hand, *it negates the right to work, and on the other hand it cancels out reproductive rights* and does not permit women to decide freely about their own reproduction" (emphasis added).[61] For Mexican groups, eliminating pregnancy screening was thus the means to ensure dual ends: the right to work *and* fulfillment of reproductive rights.[62] (See appendix 3 for an overview of specific normative references.)

Legal scholar Leticia Cuevas has analyzed the normative underpinnings for the Human Rights Watch campaign in an exhaustive 1997 report prepared for the U.S. National Administrative Office (the body responsible for managing U.S. participation in the NAFTA labor side accord).[63] Among the central normative references points were the UN Convention on the Elimination of All Forms of Discrimination against Women (CEDAW); ILO Convention 111, on Discrimination; the North American Agreement on Labor Cooperation; and article 4 of Mexico's Constitution, concerning the right to decide freely on family size and spacing of children. Mexican activists involved in the Human Rights Watch campaign accepted these normative references while also bringing the right to work in through the back door, primarily through grass-roots outreach. Mexico City feminists at the helm of the national campaign in 1998, in turn, picked up centrally on the right to work and integrated it within a broader campaign agenda aimed at deconstructing traditional notions of work and responsibility for human reproduction.

Both the Mexican Constitution and the country's Federal Labor Law characterize work as a right and a social duty, not as a commodity.[64] Mexican law echoes both regional and international conventions and treaties that include explicit provisions on the right to work, such as the American Convention on Human Rights and the CEDAW. Distinct from the United States Constitution or U.S. labor law, Mexico's system emphasizes the state's role in ensuring access to work along with employers' responsibility to favor workers who are sole wage earners for their families.[65] Article 123 of Mexico's Constitution guarantees the right to work and stipulates the right to three months of paid maternity leave. Mexican activists frequently cited it as a normative reference point. They also cited provisions on the right to work included in the Universal Declaration of Human Rights (article 23), along with provisions on nondiscrimination included in article 7.[66]

Mexican activists also differed from U.S. activists by emphasizing the social construction of the pregnancy screening problem. They viewed the practice as reflective of women's socially constructed subordination in Mexican society and highlighted deep-seated attitudes and practices that belittle women: "In our society, there is cultural discrimination against women, and frequently men (husbands, sons, bosses) abuse the power that their strength or authority confers on them and cause patrimonial, psychological or physical damage to the women and children who live with them. This discrimination is not only perpetuated at home; frequently, authorities do not attend to women as they should when women denounce a crime or demand a right—despite what our Constitution expressly says about women and men's equality before the law."[67]

Mexican activists emphasized the power of law as a catalyst in the process of social transformation. They viewed the law as a potentially "effective instrument for producing the cultural modifications that are a necessary motivation for constructing a more equitable society."[68] Political activist Elena Tapia's remarks at the opening of the 1998 Mexico City Tribunal on Reconciling Maternity and Work reflected the perspective of many individuals and groups involved in the national campaign: "[H]uman reproduction is not a women's issue—no, it is an event, a process, that implies the responsibility of all social actors. . . . [Firing for pregnancy and pregnancy screening] constitute an imminent violation of the reproductive rights of women workers. And in violating repro-ductive rights, they also constitute a violation of human rights."[69]

Similarly, in her closing remarks at the tribunal, activist María Luisa Sánchez-Fuentes observed: "For us women, the right to work is a right equal in the hierarchy to the right to the fullness of our reproductive functions and to [the right to] offer a life with dignity to our children. The reason is very simple: to be a woman is to be many things, among them worker and mother. We want society to recognize this multiple na-ture of women."[70]

Grassroots activists involved in both the Human Rights Watch cam-paign and the national-level campaign highlighted the irony of women's central role in regional and national economic development and the lack of social recognition and corresponding protections afforded them: "[W]omen confront multiple obstacles in trying to enter the world of work; they receive the worst salaries, are sexually harassed, forced to take pregnancy exams in order to get a job (violating women's right to work). If they become pregnant or have children, they are the first ones laid off from private firms and public institutions; they are the minority in director or management positions. Given that the role we women play is fundamental to the country's development process, we have not been openly valued or recognized."[71]

Penalizing women workers for pregnancy is a choice on the part of employers—a choice in which the state and society are complicit, Mexi-can activists argued. When female employees of government-run min-istries or universities are required to provide proof of nonpregnancy or when pregnant government workers are fired, the state practices out-right discrimination. When private-sector employers discriminate based on pregnancy, the state shirks its responsibility for effective monitoring of workers' rights and labor standards. Furthermore, activists argued, when pregnant women are fired and left without adequate access to health services or the means to sustain a decent life, the state has failed in its responsibility to ensure safe motherhood, placing the agents re-sponsible for society's reproduction at risk.

Although Mexico has existing domestic laws to safeguard the rights of working women and is a signatory to numerous regional and interna-tional treaties and conventions, these are rendered "dead letter" for lack of implementation, Mexican activists charged.[72] Detailed proposals for legal reform were thus central to the 1998 campaign. Activists recom-mended that key articles of the Mexican Constitution, the Federal Labor Law, and laws covering the rights of state and federal employees be re-vised to include explicit references to pregnancy-based discrimination and that safeguards for working mothers be strengthened.

For example, they proposed that specific references to pregnancy be included in article 4 (on nondiscrimination) and article 123 (on the right to work) of the Mexican Constitution.[73] Similar references are included in articles 1 and 11 of the UN Convention on the Elimination of All Forms of Discrimination against Women (CEDAW)[74] and in the final declaration and action plan of the UN International Conference on Population and Development,[75] both of which Mexico has endorsed. Activists also recommended that the Mexican government sign and ratify additional international instruments that would bind it to better implement women's rights domestically. For example, those involved in the 1998 campaign called for the signature and ratification of the 1982 ILO Convention 158, on Termination of Employment, which explicitly prohibits employment termination on grounds of pregnancy.[76]

In addition, activists proposed a wide range of institutional reforms. They called for the creation of a General Coordination Office for Equal Employment within the Secretariat of Labor and Social Protection (STPS), "to investigate and analyze discriminatory practices in employment and to propose policies to eliminate such practices." They proposed the creation of an office to oversee workplace gender discrimination within the federal Conciliation and Arbitration Board.[77] Some proposed subregional reforms, such as the creation of a statewide interdisciplinary "Cabinet for the Defense and Promotion of Reproductive Rights of Workers" in Sonora.[78] Others recommended that the mandates of state- and federal-level human rights commissions be altered to include labor rights matters.[79]

Still others called for the creation of a national database on pregnancy screening complaints and corresponding legal action. Campaign literature consistently emphasized the "difficulty of knowing how many women are affected by the problem" of pregnancy-related employment discrimination. Fully 90 percent of those affected are estimated not to file formal labor grievances, and consolidated statistics on claims filed are not available at the local, state, or national level.[80] Legal analyst Leticia Cuevas reports that researchers who surveyed officials in the Conciliation and Arbitration Boards and in the National Statistics Institute (INEGI) at the request of the US-NAO turned up "limited" to no information on the number of cases of pregnancy screening or other gender-related employment violations. "Unfortunately, the information does not exist, has not been classified, or perhaps has just not been made available," they reported.[81]

Research for this book yielded more concrete information, albeit limited: in Tijuana, the head of the local Conciliation and Arbitration Board (JCA) made an informal estimate in 2001 of the number of pregnancy screening grievances filed annually since the campaigns. At the time of the campaigns the JCA was handling an average of 3–5 pregnancy-related complaints annually. By 2001, the number of cases had increased to 10 annually. Though the number of pregnancy-related cases is small in comparison with the agency's overall caseload (the JCA handles about five thousand cases per year), the increase has nonetheless been marked.[82] In Hermosillo, independent research by Mireya Scarone-Adarga (former director of the local NGO Casa de la Mujer) confirms that 3 cases per month of firing for pregnancy are reported in Hermosillo alone, and 7 per month are reported elsewhere in the state of Sonora.[83] Activists involved in the 1998 campaign were convinced that collecting and publicizing such statistics would strengthen their efforts to promote social change.

Mexico City feminists interviewed in January 2002[84] acknowledged that while not all of these reforms were possible, there were several key victories. Among them were the creation of the Equity and Gender Policy Unit within the federal Secretariat of Labor and Social Protection (STPS) and the creation of a Mexico City–level Office for the Defense of Women's Rights. Yet several of these same feminist leaders also cautioned against undue optimism, wondering aloud about the efficiency and durability of these new institutions as well as the ability of grassroots women to exercise their rights through them.[85] As legal analyst Leticia Cuevas has pointed out: "[E]ven when discrimination is prohibited or when equality is constitutionally or legislatively guaranteed, *the effectiveness of those provisions is measured by the ability of victims to assert their constitutional and legislative rights. . . .* Rights are only claims or declarations. The notion of 'right' cannot be separated from a procedural and judicial use that gives it meaning. . . . Where there is no judicial recourse, there is nothing but words, pieces of paper" (emphasis added).[86]

Explaining the Campaigns

Why did Human Rights Watch champion the pregnancy screening issue—and why did Mexican groups, both along the border and in Mexico City, respond to the campaign with backdoor moves (as opposed to blocking ones)? Arguably, poor women working in the maquiladora industry had more pressing concerns than gender discrimination.[87] Yet this "new" issue opened a regional debate over gender discrimination that played out in the negotiating arena created by the NAFTA side accord on labor. It also set in motion debates within Mexico over economic rights and the nature of work and social reproduction. Several explanations, when "nested" together, shed light on why and how the campaigns discussed in this chapter unfolded as they did.

Rationalist Interpretation

Protectionism is occasionally invoked to explain Human Rights Watch's interest in the pregnancy screening issue. The argument runs as follows: Mexican industry competes with the United States for production and exports in an increasingly competitive global economy. The maquiladora sector, dominated by U.S. and Asian capital, is one of the most vibrant sectors of the Mexican economy; companies in the sector manufacture brand-name products for export. Human rights activists are "used" by protectionist interests in the United States (primarily labor unions) to pressure Mexican industry for labor rights reforms, particularly in the maquiladora sector. They target high-profile brand producers in the sector because these companies are familiar to American consumers, who can pressure corporations and/or the Mexican government for reforms in the maquiladora sector.

Jaime Villalpando, director of the Maquiladora Association of Tijuana, spelled out this argument in shorthand form: "These [U.S.] activists come because it's election time [in the United States] and the union is financing them. They'll leave when it's all over." Mexican groups have piggybacked on this "protectionist" agenda largely in hopes of accessing funds from U.S. unions or large, American-based NGOs. But Mexican groups are generally "too disorganized" to marshal effective follow-up efforts.[88]

However, the Mexican participants in the Human Rights Watch campaign who were interviewed for this book did not expect significant financial support—either from U.S. unions, or from Human Rights Watch—in exchange for their services or support to HRW.[89] Correspondence from HRW with key groups that assisted the organization by facilitating worker interviews or providing transportation consisted strictly of nominal reimbursement for costs incurred by those local groups in the course of assisting with Human Rights Watch's field research.[90] Nor were the Mexican feminists at the helm of the 1998 national campaign motivated solely by potential financial gain. Although members of these groups did tap external donor funds (i.e., the Dutch bilateral grant and MacArthur Foundation individual funds) and were able to persuade the Mexico City Human Rights Commission to lend in-kind support to their campaign, the material support that Mexican feminist groups received was modest at best.

Indeed, the motivation for Mexican groups to participate in the campaigns was more complex than narrow financial gain. In Mexico, border-based NGOs and networks face particular political, financial, and social challenges. The country's strong tradition of presidentialism and the centralization of power under the Revolutionary Institutional Party (PRI) for nearly all of the twentieth century resulted in an extraordinary concentration of power in the center of Mexico, quite literally. The capital, Mexico City, is where decisions are made, programs funded, policies determined, trends set; in a geographically vast country, the border and capital are literally thousands of miles apart. The capital is the place civil-society-based organizations have developed most widely. As Blanca Torres, a Mexican analyst, explains, there has been a "historical lack" of labor and environmental NGOs in the northern border region: "Groups in the center have had better funding."[91]

The northern border, by contrast, is a region of significant transience: internal migration to the region from other parts of Mexico (and from Central America) is considerable. People come to the border in search of work, often with the intention of crossing (legally or illegally) into the United States in search of a better life. Far away from their home communities, lacking networks of support, many people at the grassroots level are not inclined to form or join civil society organizations. They lack the time, energy, resources, or social incentive to do so.[92]

Activists on the northern border, in turn, complain that their work is perennially underfunded, politically marginalized (or, worse still, ignored completely) by political actors in the center of the country—and beyond. In an era of cross-border activism and deepening relations between Mexico and its two northern neighbors, U.S. groups often "leapfrog" over groups at the border to foster ties with Mexico City–based groups. Arturo Solís, director of a Reynosa-based human rights group, explained: "[I]nternational organizations often use groups in Mexico City and forget about those of us who are here involved in the work, participating in it. . . . [T]he groups in Mexico City use information produced by those of us who aren't there, and international organizations normally dedicate themselves to the groups in Mexico City and forget about us."[93]

The Human Rights Watch campaign offered NGOs along the northern border the potential leverage of this influential group's name and reputation. An affiliation with HRW heightened the chances that local policymakers would respond to claims and that the local press and public would pay attention to economic rights and gender issues. With greater policy impact and public attention might ultimately come more funding. Indeed, activists hoped the Human Rights Watch connection would counter the "leapfrogging effect" and thus strengthen border-based groups' hands vis-à-vis NGOs and political actors in the center of Mexico.

Julia Quiñónez of the CFO cited such leverage as an explicit reason for participating in the campaign:

> When groups from different countries are involved, there's more coverage, more interest on the part of the local press. As you know, Mexico is a really subordinated country, especially vis-à-vis the United States; when the United States has a cold, Mexico gets pneumonia. . . . *[A]s long as it's just Mexican organizations, our government is going to try to justify and not accept the situation. But when there's collaboration with groups from other countries, the government gets worried. . . .* After the Human Rights Watch campaign, people listened to us a lot. . . . It got an international reaction. (Emphasis added)[94]

Carmen Valadéz of Factor X similarly noted: "[T]he fact that an international human rights organization was paying attention to something here was really important for us. And this gave us more strength. . . . Before, we were small groups of workers who talked about this. But we didn't have a lot of authority."[95]

Feminist groups based in Mexico City also had rationally based motivations for launching their campaign. Throughout the 1990s, these groups fought both for the right to legalized abortion and for an end to violence against women. As Patricia Mercado, a leading political activist, explained, championing the cause of pregnant women afforded groups in the Mexican feminist movement an opportunity to critically refine their image: "I was already working on the theme of abortion— and *one of the things we thought strategically was that it's important for those of us who are seen in defense of abortion to also be seen as in defense of women who are being fired for pregnancy.* We have to be as firmly in defense of one as the other. Finally, it's about women's right to choose" (emphasis added).[96] These, then, were some of the rationalist motivations underlying activism on the anti-pregnancy-screening campaigns of the late 1990s. But other factors also played a role.

Structural Interpretation

In the United States, the dominant legislative and social conception of human rights is a civil and political one. This emphasis is mirrored in the NAFTA side accord on labor. The rights at issue are defined narrowly in civil and political terms; their implementation is the responsibility of states parties to the NAFTA and its side agreement on labor. And the aim is to implement existing law, not to frame new rights.

The National Administration Offices created under the terms of the labor side accord are mandated to address labor rights protection and promotion along these lines. Operationally, their activities are linked to each country's respective ministry or department of labor—not to state agencies responsible for social policy planning and execution. There is no reference to broader social welfare legislation included in the side accord. Neither Mexico nor Canada nor the United States was willing to yield its sovereignty in social policymaking to the oversight of a transnational body, such as the offices monitoring the NAALC in each country.

Hence, a structural interpretation of this case would explain Human Rights Watch's decision to opt for a campaign focused on nondiscrimination as one constrained by the juridical bounds of the labor side accord.

By contrast, the 1917 Mexican Constitution enshrines work as both a social right and a duty.[97] Itself the product of a revolution in which upward of 10 percent of all Mexicans lost their lives, the Constitution includes a labor bill of rights (article 123) that was among the most progressive of its time when drafted.[98] The conception of work as both right and duty has influenced the legislative and popular cultures of Mexico. The country's Federal Labor Law (LFT) includes sections on both, and activists have considered economic and social rights a valid focus for human rights advocacy.[99] Popular education materials produced by NGOs involved in labor rights advocacy in Mexico reflect the LFT's dual emphasis on rights and responsibilities. For example, the Coalition for Justice in the Maquiladoras (a binational network of activists) has produced a two-volume set of training booklets on the LFT; one focuses on rights, the other responsibilities. The former includes a section on the rights of pregnant workers.[100]

But in practice, labor rights became increasingly divided from human rights during the 1990s in Mexico. Constitutional reforms made under then-president Carlos Salinas de Gortari in the early 1990s created a complex system of national human rights ombuds offices but officially separated human rights from labor rights by leaving the latter out of the mandate of the new human rights institutions. Article 102(B) of the Mexican Constitution explicitly prevents state-level human rights commissions from addressing labor violations, as well as judicial or electoral matters. Corresponding law covering the mandate of the National Human Rights Commission (adopted 29 June 1992) prevents the commission itself from considering labor matters and directly refers in its own Article 3 to constitutional article 102(B).[101]

Supporters of the existing separation of labor rights from wider human rights mandates argue that other government institutions charged with protecting labor rights—such as the Office of the Labor Inspector and the Conciliation and Arbitration Boards—were already in existence when the human rights commissions were created, and hence it would not have made sense to mandate the *new* human rights offices to take over the function of these existing labor rights institutions. Nor would it have been practical, they argue: Mexico is a poor country and must prioritize its rights concerns, beginning with civil and political rights. Economic and social rights will come with development, the argument runs.[102]

However, opponents of the theoretical and functional division among human rights argue in favor of *including* labor rights within the mandate of Mexico's human rights commissions at the state and federal level. Raúl Ramírez, the human rights ombudsman for the state of Baja California, has advocated this position:

> The principal task for the modern ombudsman in the millennium just opening is to make the indivisible character of human rights visible. . . . Social rights are norms. But times of crisis are precisely when there is little to distribute. For some, the answer is to wait for better times; for us, the recognition and satisfaction of social rights cannot be postponed: it is ethically and morally necessary to fight for the juridical protection and sociopolitical organization that guarantees the *minimum* rights of the population—above all, of the neediest groups. Truly, this is our challenge.[103]

Indeed, since the introduction of article 102(B), Mexican activists have challenged the separation of rights by organizing explicitly "integrated" human rights campaigns. The backdoor moves by Mexican activists on the "receiving end" of the Human Rights Watch campaign could thus be interpreted as emerging in response to the broader structure of the new Mexican human rights regime.

The structure of Mexican labor law could also be interpreted as a factor shaping the 1998 campaign launched by Mexico City–based feminist organizations and framed around new concepts of work and of responsibility for human reproduction. First adopted in 1931, Mexico's Federal Labor Law has been only minimally revised since then; revisions are currently in progress. As it stands, the law reflects traditionally gendered parenting roles: women are assumed to be not only the bearers of children but also their primary caregivers. Regulations on maternity and childcare are grouped together in the LFT under the heading "Women's Work."[104] The act of bearing children is also assumed to take women "out of" a state of productivity; the medical certificate legally required to obtain maternity leave and corresponding benefits is commonly referred to as a "certificate of incapacity." Mexican feminists thus sought to challenge the very structure of Mexican labor law.

Changes in the nature of the Mexican economy were also a structural factor affecting the nature of grassroots activism within Mexico. Particularly along the northern border, activists were quick to point out that Mexico's Federal Labor Law is inadequate to protect workers as the country moves toward flexible production and takes the corresponding steps of cutting (or at least thinning) the social safety net while basing benefits on productivity, not entitlements. Under this rubric, productivity is measured in terms of numbers of units produced, and benefits are meted out accordingly—not in terms of the embedded sets of social relationships and the networks of mutual obligation and reciprocity.

A wide range of structural factors thus influenced the development of the campaigns discussed in this chapter: the historic emphasis on economic rights and the contemporary reality of a growing labor rights/ human rights divide in Mexico; the structure of Mexico's Federal Labor Law and its incongruities with modern gender roles, industrial trends, and the corresponding social pressures they generate. But there are additional factors to consider.

Social Movement Interpretation

Insights from social movement theory also help explain why and how the Human Rights Watch campaign and the succeeding 1998 national campaign unfolded. The creation of the NAFTA side accord on labor presented activists with a new political opportunity. They mobilized allies from across sectors and across borders (in the first case) as well as throughout Mexico (in the second) to launch the campaigns discussed in this chapter. Human Rights Watch framed its efforts in terms of civil and political rights alone, while local activists in Mexico incorporated additional messages on economic rights and the responsibility of society for human reproduction into their grassroots outreach.

Outside political opportunities (such as the NAFTA/NAALC) served as a significant catalyst for Human Rights Watch, but so, too, were internal organizational changes. In 1990, Human Rights Watch had created its own Women's Rights Program division.[105] Staff members in that division were eager to explore new tools for gender rights advocacy—and the NAALC offered one. Their efforts and the resulting reports and campaign on Submission 9701 provided Mexican labor rights and feminist activists with a political opportunity. Submission 9701 put pregnancy screening on the map internationally, and Mexican activists used that international attention to pressure their government for domestic reforms. Pregnancy screening in Mexico's maquiladoras became the focus of bilateral discussions between President Salinas de Gortari and President Clinton.[106] Both the 1998 and 1999 U.S. State Department country reports on Mexico referenced pregnancy screening.[107] And the issue spurred related discussion in both the 1998 and 1999 sessions of the UN Committee on the Elimination of All Forms of Discrimination against Women (CEDAW) and the 1999 session of the UN Committee on the Rights of the Child.[108]

The mobilization structures for both the Human Rights Watch campaign and the 1998 national-level campaign that followed it were also in place. Activists drew on preexisting connections among groups that had struggled against the passage of the NAFTA. Formal binational coalitions had emerged as early as 1989—among them, the Coalition for Justice in the Maquiladoras—and regional networks along the northern border had also emerged, including the Comité Fronterizo de Obreras. Members of both of these networks took an active role in the Human Rights Watch campaign against pregnancy screening.

Feminists networks were in place, too, and were already focused on issues of reproductive rights. Despite the center-periphery gaps discussed above and the challenge of mobilizing people across the vast distances, groups from throughout the border region had established some connections with Mexico City–based human rights groups and feminist networks by the 1990s. Women unionists, for example had forged ties through the network of Mujeres en Acción Sindical (Women in Union Action, or MAS).[109] International donor organizations, such as the MacArthur Foundation and Ford Foundation, had fostered capacity building among Mexican women's networks at the national and subregional level.[110] Such networks were crucial in moving each campaign forward and carrying out follow-up, where possible.

Framing was the most creative aspect of either campaign. Human Rights Watch framed its campaign in civil and political rights terms in keeping with its repertoire of contention: in-depth reporting coupled with high-profile denunciations of human rights abuse that states either sponsor or fail to prevent, plus use of the media to fan public condemnation and focus political attention on the offending government.[111] Local groups in the northern border region centered on economic rights claims, while feminists in Mexico City pushed for alternative conceptions of gendered work and family responsibilities. Though all opposed to pregnancy screening, each set of actors characterized and contextualized the problem distinctly; their differing normative discourses reflected these varying emphases, as did their distinct activities on the ground.

Synthesis

Rational, structural, and social movement factors together influenced the unfolding of the various campaigns against pregnancy screening discussed in this chapter. Framing was the central act that most clearly revealed the combined effect of these factors, and backdoor moves were the mechanism within the framing process that Mexican activists employed to maneuver additional human rights issues into the campaign arena.

Human Rights Watch was straightforward in framing its campaign from a civil and political rights perspective. Structural factors—chief among them, the scope of the NAALC's mandate—coupled with the organization's own repertoire of contention influenced the scope of the frame. Human Rights Watch had no need to employ backdoor moves, since it launched the campaign and set the opening frame. Mexican border-based activists who took part in the HRW campaign did not try to widen this official frame. Instead, they brought economic rights issues in through the back door, at the grassroots level.

Although the scope of the labor side accord's mandate restricted the "official" negotiating agenda to civil and political rights concerns, local Mexican activists involved in this campaign at the grassroots level committed themselves to spreading the message of economic rights, a message that resonated with their own priorities and repertoire of contention.

Feminists based in Mexico City, in turn, launched a campaign in 1998 that capitalized opportunely on the political space opened by the Human Rights Watch campaign. Feminists incorporated Human Rights Watch's emphasis on discrimination (framed in civil and political terms) and moved beyond it, openly framing their campaign in much broader terms. Rather than introduce themes through the back door, feminists introduced them directly. They insisted on the right to work (already brought in by groups at the border), while also challenging the dominant Mexican conception of work itself.

What kept activists from simply blocking human rights messages that were out of sync with their own normative understandings, as they did in the Bangladesh case? Why did Mexican activists make backdoor moves at all?

Two factors significantly influenced the decision to make backdoor moves: the first was the dual-target nature of the campaign's emergence. Distinct from an "outside-in" campaign, a dual-target campaign focuses on actors in multiple countries or settings. Dual targeting increases the chance that activists launching a campaign will gain buy-in from allies in the target country, because this type of campaign conveys the impression of even-handedness. It also increases the possibility that allies will gain something from the campaign because the scope of the intended targets is broader. The dual nature of the anti-pregnancy-screening campaigns discussed in this chapter—the fact that each targeted more than one country or sector—was part of their appeal to activists from both the United States and Mexico. In contrast to the Bangladesh case (which was largely an "outside-in" campaign), the anti-pregnancy-screening campaigns quickly generated a high level of internal (i.e., Mexican) support from the groups within the targeted country. Innovations in framing helped those groups to "sell" the campaign to their own local audiences, in turn.

A second important factor that influenced the decision to make backdoor moves was the nature of shared interests among activists on the sending and receiving ends of the campaign. Activists who determine that there is more to be gained from surmounting their differences and collaborating are likely to do so, rather than block. Collaborating does not erase differences among groups (either material or normative), but it can minimize the appearance of conflict, which in turn enables activists to present a common front against their opposition.

In this case study, Human Rights Watch needed the grassroots testimony of women workers in order to build a case against pregnancy screening; hence, the organization invited border-based groups to participate in its investigation and later in the dissemination of its reports. Groups along the U.S.-Mexico border had to surmount longstanding rivalries among themselves in order to take part in the HRW investigation and campaign. They also had to surmount rivalries with Mexico City–based groups in order to take part in the 1998 national-level campaign on reconciling maternity and work. Groups in Mexico City, in turn, incorporated economic rights themes and invited border-based groups to take part in the 1998 campaign because they wanted to capitalize on the attention already garnered by groups working on the pregnancy screening issue in the *maquila* industry—while widening the lens further to focus on the social construction of work and reproductive responsibilities.

All of the parties involved in these campaigns needed one another. The tradeoffs each was willing to make in framing the agenda differed. Human Rights Watch made the fewest compromises because it had the financial resources and political capital to launch a campaign focused on civil and political rights with considerable likelihood of success. The organization was not totally insensitive to the interests of local partners, but it did keep the focus on civil and political rights issues in the interest of advancing Submission 9701 through the NAALC process and in keeping with its own repertoire of contention.

For Mexican groups along the border, backdoor moves (rather than blocking) made sense because the Human Rights Watch campaign offered these groups more leverage with government (U.S. and Mexican) and business actors than they would have had without participating. Similarly, for Mexico City feminists, incorporating discrimination and economic rights concerns from other activists' work on the pregnancy screening issue was the best way to build on existing political momentum while at the same time introducing even deeper proposals for social change.

Activists involved in these campaigns were united by their mutual interest in shaming the parties responsible for pregnancy testing into reform. Where they differed was in how they "named" the nature of human rights abuse. The distinct slogans used by activists reflect critical differences in the way they framed rights: "A job or your rights" for Human Rights Watch, "Economic justice and the mirage of the *maquilas*" for border-based Mexican groups, and "Human reproduction, a social responsibility" for Mexico City feminists. Some (i.e., Human Rights Watch) took as their point of departure the traditional notion of workplace discrimination based on gender. Others (i.e., groups along the border) brought in through the back door a concern for the impact of such discrimination on the right to work. Still others (i.e., Mexico City feminists) picked up on these "front" and "backdoor" concerns and integrated them within a broader challenge to the patriarchal economic and social structures of Mexican law and society. The intertwined campaigns offer rich terrain for inquiry into the nature of norms change and special insights into backdoor moves as a central mechanism in this process.

5

A Decade Later

Assessing Advocacy's Effects over Time

I
t has been close to ten years since the end of the campaigns discussed
in this book. Did the millions of dollars in program funds in the
Bangladesh case make a difference in the lives of working children?
Did the hundreds of hours of research and testimony in the Mexico case
directly affect the lives of working women in that country?

More generally, how do transnational labor rights campaigns like
these relate to broader changes in human rights advocacy in the 1990s
and beyond? Did these campaigns have a significant impact on how policymakers, popular sector actors, business leaders, or academics understand child rights, labor rights, or the dynamics of gender and economic
rights? Have national, regional, or international institutions taken action
in any way as a result of these campaigns? Has government or corporate
policy or action changed? Have social attitudes changed?

This chapter analyzes both the Bangladesh and Mexico cases, exploring
their practical impact while simultaneously tying this analysis to a broader
discussion of human rights norms evolution in the 1990s and beyond. The
first section, on case-specific impact, is organized in terms of three contrasting pairs of concepts, informed by the work of Jonathan Fox:[1]

Outside/inside dynamics

- What was the impact on the target? (Did either campaign transform
  related government policy at the national, regional or international

level? Affect the behavior of private sector actors? Affect public attitudes?)
- What was the impact on the campaign itself? (Were there changes in
organizing strategies or political culture?)

Material/nonmaterial aspects

- What were the material/tangible concessions?
- What were the discursive/intangible concessions?

Intentional/unintentional impact

- What were the intended consequences?
- What were the unintended consequences?

Part of the challenge of assessing impact is that doing so naturally
forces us to think in terms of counterfactuals: What would have happened in the absence of these campaigns? How might these situations
have turned out differently if activists had never launched campaigns in
either setting? As Fox has asked: "What 'counts' as making a difference? . . . What would have happened without binational campaigning?
Perhaps the state of human rights violations did not get much better, but
then again maybe it would have gotten worse in the absence of transnational campaigning."[2]

Evaluating the Impact of
the Bangladesh Campaign

The Harkin bill campaign and subsequent consumer boycott, along
with the responses these provoked within Bangladesh, have been widely
analyzed in scholarly and policy literatures. The following analysis employs Fox's three-level rubric to explore the campaign's effects on multiple levels.

Outside/Inside Dynamics: Impact on Targets

Since the mid-1990s, business and government in Bangladesh have
publicly adopted an "abolitionist line" on child labor. The website of the
Bangladesh Garment Manufacturers and Exporters Association
(BGMEA) claims that the association has "responded to the international
requirement of elimination of child labor from the garment sector of
Bangladesh and has successfully achieved the objective" by participat-

ing in factory monitoring programs, in keeping with the terms of the memorandum of understanding (MOU) signed in July 1995.[3]

The MOU has repeatedly been cast as a positive achievement by members of Bangladesh's business community and government and by leading economic policy think tanks such as the Dhaka-based Centre for Policy Dialogue. Particularly as Bangladesh faced the January 2005 phaseout of textile quotas previously available under the Multifiber Agreement (MFA) of the General Agreement on Tariffs and Trade—a potentially devastating economic blow for the country—it became more urgent to "sell" the experience of the MOU in order to persuade international business to remain in the country despite the allure of other markets. As the Centre for Policy Dialogue's main study on the issue argued: "One of the major successes of the RMG [ready-made garment] sector is the way Bangladesh tackled the child labour issue. . . . This success should be highlighted as a sign of Bangladesh's sincerity in addressing all social issues related to the workers in the sector."[4]

The government of Bangladesh has aligned itself with other countries in South Asia in calling for an "end" to child labor in hazardous occupations by 2000 and elimination of child labor as a whole by 2010. In 1996, leaders of the South Asian Association for Regional Cooperation (SAARC) met in Pakistan and together adopted the Rawalpindi Resolution,[5] which set out these time-bound targets. Background notes to the Rawalpindi Resolution itself cite an even earlier call by regional governments for the "progressive and accelerated elimination of child labour"—namely, the 1992 SAARC Colombo Resolution on Children. Specific time-bound targets, however, first appear in the Rawalpindi Resolution.

Bangladesh has since cited the Rawalpindi Resolution in its own official policy statements on child labor—namely, in its second periodic report to the UN Committee on the Rights of the Child (CRC), the treaty-monitoring body for the UN Convention on the Rights of the Child, to which Bangladesh is a signatory.[6] (As is typical with many reports submitted by states parties to the UN treaty-monitoring bodies, Bangladesh's second periodic report to the UN Committee on the Rights of the Child was considerably delayed: due in 1997, it was submitted in 2001 and finally taken up by the CRC in 2003.)

The Rawalpindi Resolution seems to challenge one of the main arguments of this book—namely, that an economic-rights-centered understanding of children's rights emerged in Bangladesh following the Harkin bill campaign, as a result of blocking moves made by local activists. Instead, the Rawalpindi Resolution's targets would seem to be more in line with the Northern view that child labor can ultimately be eliminated than with the Southern child rights perspective that emerged in some quarters within Bangladesh during the Harkin bill campaign.

But the abolitionist discourse on child labor adopted by the government of Bangladesh has not been translated into practice. The government may be calling officially for the abolition of child labor in part to buttress its chances of attracting business in the wake of the MFA phase-out and in part because rhetoric is cheaper than actually allocating the resources necessary to achieve such good intentions. Words buy time, in essence. The following evidence buttresses this interpretation.

Several in-depth academic and policy analyses appeared in the two to three years after the MOU was signed,[7] and the government of Bangladesh carried out its first comprehensive survey of child labor from 1995 through 1996. The Bangladesh Bureau of Statistics established a baseline for critically assessing the nature and scope of child labor in the country and proposed "future regular collection of data on working children . . . through the incorporation of a child labour component in the two-yearly labour force survey and ten-yearly national census."[8] Yet as recently as 2001, Bangladesh still had "no national policy on child labor," despite its allegiance to the Rawalpindi Resolution, as the government itself acknowledged in reports to the UN Committee on the Rights of the Child. While noting that "the ILO is providing support for the formulation of a child labour policy," the government also noted that "additional resources . . . [have] not been available to fulfill this commitment to date."[9]

There are references (albeit limited) to child work in both the first and second periodic reports submitted by Bangladesh to the UN Committee on the Rights of the Child. In the first report (due in 1992 and submitted in 1995), the government of Bangladesh included both a section on education with references to specific programs aimed at meeting the needs of "poor working children," and a section on child labor itself. The report noted that the activities of one NGO, the Underprivileged Children's Educational Program (UCEP), aimed to "improve the socioeconomic status" of working children "through its employment support component, proper employment of its target group following their education and training. For this purpose, UCEP established 'dynamic linkage' with employers, especially in the private sector."[10] The child labor section of Bangladesh's initial report to the CRC refers primarily to children's work in the household and notes that some children work for "reasons of survival," but includes only a short discussion of industrial work, arguing that "formal employment in the industrial sector is limited in Bangladesh and there is such a vast supply of unskilled labourers that the inducement to use children is not very great among employers."[11]

The Harkin bill campaign, however, changed the nature of debate completely. The campaign demonstrated that in certain industrial sectors of Bangladesh, children were in fact employed. The high-profile status of child garment workers, in particular, caused Bangladeshi garment manufacturers to distance themselves completely from any association with child labor over the next several years.

By the time the government of Bangladesh prepared its second periodic report to the CRC (due in 1997, submitted in 2001, and taken up in 2003), the position on child labor had thus become more nuanced. The opening paragraph of the second periodic report refers directly to the Rawalpindi Resolution and restates the government's commitment to the abolition of child labor. Yet subsequent sections distinguish between types of child work—for example, domestic service (employers are urged to allow children who work as house servants to have time off for study, rest, play, and contact with family members) and heavy work (the report advises that it be prohibited).[12] Thus the report implicitly acknowledges that child work will continue and should be regulated in some way, despite its opening salvo that child work should be abolished entirely by 2010.

Indeed, SAARC's own background notes to the Rawalpindi Resolution acknowledge the general contradiction between what South Asian governments say about child labor and what they do: "Public commitment to the legal protection of children is reflected in the framing of national legislation which exists in all South Asian countries. *In general, child labour is not prohibited; rather, it is sought to be regulated. . . . In all countries of the region, there is a contradiction between the law and its practice.* Implementation and consistent enforcement pose serious constraints. Breach of laws rarely results in prosecution and stiff penalties" (emphasis added).[13]

Some observers have argued that the 1990s were a period in which developing country governments like Bangladesh's and those of other SAARC countries found themselves with little alternative but to adopt the Western line on child labor—an abolitionist line[14]—because they had few resources to develop alternative programs for working children on their own. They needed the funds available through international aid (ideological strings attached) and so adopted a corresponding goal of eliminating child labor. The threat of trade sanctions also acted as a strong incentive to do so. As scholar Ben White has explained: "[T]he promotion by powerful lobbying organizations of boycotts or sanctions by governments or groups of government in the West against the import of products made with child labour, coupled with parallel efforts by non-governmental organizations to promote consumer boycotts of such products . . . make it highly inadvisable for any exporting country to acknowledge the existence of children's employment at all, for example by protective legislation or other efforts to promote the improvement of children's working conditions."[15]

For the government of Bangladesh as for other countries in South Asia, adopting the Rawalpindi Resolution—and then letting enforcement slide—may in fact have been a conscious strategy. It was easiest to agree in principle with the need to abolish child labor in order to attain much-needed development support, but then to tread water domestically in service of this goal.[16] Committing to the abolition of child labor by 2010 may not have been realistic, but it lessened the threat of trade sanctions, increased the likelihood of related development assistance, and bought time for South Asian governments like Bangladesh's to focus on other, more pressing policy concerns.

The external pressure of the Harkin bill and corresponding anti-child-labor campaign thus had multiple effects. It had one effect on the business sector in Bangladesh: it pushed business to dismiss children en masse, then to block and threaten its own countercampaign against U.S. importers, and finally to adopt an abolitionist line as publicly evident from the "child free" marketing push of the BGMEA. Yet even six years after the MOU was struck—in 2001, as the Centre for Policy Dialogue in Dhaka gathered business, government, union, and NGO representatives to discuss the impending phaseout of the MFA—business leaders were still visceral in their resentment of the overall approach of the Harkin bill campaign. One garment manufacturer complained:

> Often, they forget that cutting of [sic] one's head can't be a solution to headache . . . rather, those campaign groups are the worst violators of human rights for whose high-sounding principles, illogical regulations are imposed on industries leading to their eventual collapse. . . . We have a lot of positive aspects to portray before the international community. Elimination of child labour from the RMG [ready-made garment] sector is one such issue which may be projected as a success story.[17]

The Harkin bill campaign had a similar effect on the government of Bangladesh: it pushed government to adopt an abolitionist line on child labor publicly (in regional and international forums). And it had yet another effect on civil society organizations in Bangladesh: it pushed local NGOs, child rights advocates, and Bangladeshi intellectuals to reject outside interference directly, to block and launch a countercampaign focused on a broader conception of human rights than the "abolitionist" perspective, and in turn to develop a child-rights-centered framework.

Outside/Inside Dynamics: Impact on the Campaign Itself

The most obvious effect of this campaign was to empower local activists in Bangladesh to send an alternative human rights message distinct from that put forward by mainstream groups at the helm of the human rights movement in the United States. Yet as discussed in chapter 3, there were fissures within the "southern" community of activists: Bangladeshi Roman Catholic nun Rosaline Costa—who initially sought help from U.S. allies much along the lines of the "boomerang" model developed by Keck and Sikkink—embraced the "northern," "abolitionist" perspective, and local activists roundly rejected her and organized a countercampaign instead. In doing so, they blocked the dominant human rights discourse of the Harkin bill campaign (which emphasized abolishing child labor) and replaced it with emphasis on children's right to work.

The evolution of an alternative child rights focus, in turn, spawned a child-rights-centered development paradigm and corresponding NGO policy action in Bangladesh in the years following the signing of the MOU in 1995. Today, the child rights movement in Bangladesh is animated more by concerns about the identity dimension of child rights than by the poverty aspect, as will be discussed shortly.

Material Aspects

The Bangladesh case has received very mixed reviews for its social welfare impact. Though the sentiment behind the Harkin bill may have been admirable—namely, the desire to help children—critics argue that these good intentions did nothing to address the fate of tens of thousands of children dismissed from work and never located for inclusion in the schooling and stipend programs created under the MOU.[18]

As noted in chapter 3, the Bangladesh MOU had the immediate effect of reducing the number of children working in the garment industry significantly: the overall numbers diminished from 43 percent of BGMEA factories employing children to 3 percent in six years (as indicated by random monitoring carried out from 1995 to 2001).[19] So the impact on the intended targets—the Bangladeshi garment industry and the government of Bangladesh—was significant. And the children identified in the post-MOU initial survey—roughly ten thousand of them—were eligible for stipends and schooling. The 1996 background notes to the Rawalpindi Resolution point out that twenty-five hundred nonformal schools were established in Bangladesh "to meet the needs of these children."[20]

But critics have argued that the MOU projects were overly ambitious, marked by poor planning and coordination and spurred on by consumer and political (i.e., American) pressure to "do something" rather than necessarily to do what was best for the children concerned. In particular, longstanding concerns about the quality, sustainability, and appropriateness of the stipends and schooling provided under the MOU surfaced in the midterm reporting on the MOU and were later echoed in final evaluations of the program, discussed shortly.

For example, midterm internal evaluations noted the continuing challenge of underwriting the stipend component of the program. Rijk van Haarlem, then director of the ILO/IPEC program in Bangladesh, urged: "If we include stipends in a programme, we have to be sure we can *afford* to do so. Otherwise, we have to seek other, *more sustainable solutions* for income generation and maintenance, like skill training and micro-credit schemes."[21] Sheena Crawford, a British academic who has since evaluated the Bangladesh case, notes that while the MOU "has provided some models for future projects . . . *paying stipends will never be sustainable*" (emphasis added).[22]

And scholar Gayatri Spivak has criticized the schooling component of the MOU, in particular, arguing that the type of education provided was wholly inadequate to the children's needs: "[T]he 'education' to be provided is materially useless, because it is in no way continuous with the national education system. . . . My own direct involvement is with the nature, quality, effectiveness, and relevance of the teaching in ground-level schools. I can say with conviction that those questions cannot be raised in the hapless situation that follows the so-called restoration of the sanctity of childhood at the direct foreign investment factories."[23] A senior staff member of the International Labour Organization (ILO), interviewed in 1997, reflected critically:

> What we have done here in Bangladesh is described as fantastic. I wonder how fantastic it really is. How much difference will these two or three years in school make to these children? In three years, the [factory] helper could have been an operator, with better pay and more savings. Even if the manufacturers keep their word and give them back their jobs at the end of their schooling, the Memorandum [of Understanding] children will hardly be better off, while their peers will have gotten on with their careers. We have spent millions of dollars on 8,000 children. The money itself could have transformed their lives. This is an experiment by the donors, and the Bangladeshi children have to pay.[24]

Beginning in 2000–2001, the UN Children's Fund (UNICEF) and the ILO's International Programme on the Elimination of Child Labour

(IPEC) initiated separate reviews of the Bangladesh MOU. The former was an in-depth analysis of the overall impact on children of the agreement, whereas the ILO/IPEC study was a narrower project evaluation focusing solely on the IPEC components of the projects funded under the agreement. The two agencies formed a "joint technical advisory group" in 2002 and worked toward releasing a synthesis report along with their own agency reports on 14 September 2004 in Dhaka, Bangladesh.[25]

Both reports assess only post-1995 (i.e., post MOU) outcomes, *not* the condition of children dismissed before the MOU was signed and thus not included in the corresponding MOU schooling and stipend programs. The mass dismissals of these children prior to the MOU and their fate are the source of much criticism within Bangladesh and internationally. Nevertheless, the reports are both extremely in-depth and candid about the performance of the MOU programs created after 1995. Among the key findings:

- Despite the pioneering nature of the MOU collaboration, the project has failed to generate stakeholder buy-in,[26] which in turn puts its sustainability into jeopardy. The BGMEA has still not paid $80,000 of its promised contribution, arguing it cannot afford to do so in the wake of the industry's struggles against global competition given the 2005 MFA quota phaseout.[27] Nor has the industry association developed the capacity to monitor factories independently, continuing to rely on government and ILO assistance.
- Fully 80 percent of the children in the UNICEF survey "reported that their food consumption was reduced when they lost their jobs in the garment industry. Losing a job also affected their access to health care and treatment. The assessment found that no major differences were seen in consumption patterns in the long term, however."[28]
- Around 1 percent of the children surveyed by UNICEF reported awareness of young female workers dismissed and going into prostitution. Overall, however, the number of ex-garment-worker children going into hazardous work—including sex work—is "probably much less than was portrayed in the media."[29]
- One-third (31 percent) of the children identified for inclusion in MOU programs received education, 7 percent received skills training, and 1.6 percent of the children's families received microcredit assistance. "Regular interactions by monitors with beneficiaries" was found to contribute "to low drop-out rates and successful investments"[30] among those reached by the programs.

- Despite questions about the nature of informal schooling and how well it prepares children for life in the working world, the agencies found that "children with only a few years of school still fare better than those who do not go to school at all. The value of education is acknowledged but it needs to be properly tailored to children's specific needs." Indeed, an "overwhelming majority (85%) of children enrolled in an MOU school would have preferred a combination of earning and learning."[31]

Nonmaterial/Discursive Aspects

The final evaluations of the MOU jointly released in 2004 by UNICEF and the ILO termed the agreement one of the "best-known child labour interventions of the last decade. It had wider significance concerning what is best for working children with much subsequent debate around the notion of the MOU programme as a model. Additionally, the attention that the MOU programme received both nationally and globally helped put the child labour issue on the map at the end of the 1990s."[32] But how was this debate shaped and what were its effects on understandings of child rights within the campaign itself and beyond?

In the years since the Harkin bill campaign and resulting MOU, policy debate and popular activism on child labor internationally have continued to evolve in several directions. The main thrust of multilateral policy action has been on the "worst forms" of child labor. The ILO passed Convention 182 (on the worst forms of child labor) in 1998, while UNICEF focused its programming in the 1990s on child protection with special emphasis on two new protocols to the UN Convention on the Rights of the Child (one on prevention of child trafficking and another on child soldiers) that entered into force in 2002.[33]

Key grassroots campaigns, such as the Global March on Child Labor, have mirrored the emphasis on child protection and coupled it with activism on the right to education. This civil society network, which initially formed in preparation for a 1998 march on the ILO during the discussion stages of ILO 182, has since sustained a high level of popular involvement internationally from citizens in developing and industrialized countries. Over time, it has broadened its focus to include a "global campaign for education," carried out with the support of major American and European NGOs, unions, and public service organizations.[34]

Yet a significant movement of working children themselves also emerged in the 1990s, and its members insist on their "right to work"— clashing with the Global March.[35] Coalitions of working children under the umbrella of the International Movement of Working Children argued for their right to give input on the drafting of ILO 182. While "fighting every day against hazardous work and against exploitation of child work," they have argued that they are also fighting for "the improvement of life and working conditions of all children in the world. We want all the children in the world to have, one day, the right to make a choice between working and not working. Work should be in accordance with the capacity and development of each and every child and not depend on his/her age."[36]

The perspective of the working children's movement challenges both the notion of fixed minimum standards (e.g., on age) central to international labor law and the concept of child protection central to most international policy formulation on the issue. The fact that child workers are demanding the right to work—coupled with the call by some to be allowed to exercise the right to unionize—has also provoked controversy within the advocacy community and in policy circles.[37]

Within Bangladesh, the Harkin bill campaign and the MOU had the effect of solidifying the focus on child rights. In 2000, British academic Sarah C. White carried out a field study in Bangladesh involving representatives of thirteen development agencies and sixty disadvantaged children (i.e., current and former child workers). Without referring directly to the Harkin bill campaign and subsequent MOU, White's findings nevertheless highlighted a key trend in Bangladesh in the 1990s related to NGO discourse and corresponding policy action on child rights: White found that the "language of child rights now dominates" development policy and that the thrust of the proposed "remedy lies not in addressing the structures that produce (child) poverty, but in convincing parents, employers, civil society and the state that children constitute a distinct social group with specific rights. . . . [This] is perhaps not surprising, since using the language of rights has become virtually a prerequisite for the receipt of donor funding. In practice, however, many of the [NGO-led] programmes were mainly directed at child welfare."[38]

In other words, a "two-level game"[39] may be in evidence, in which Bangladeshi development agencies have crafted a public discourse on children's rights aimed at emphasizing the identity of working children (and garnering international funding for related programs), yet have carried out practical programs aimed at addressing the children's poverty. White is critical of the practical impact this strategy has had on poor children: "The gap between the rights they have in CRC [Convention on the Rights of the Child] theory and the realities of their practical experience was simply too great for the children. Instead of being 'empowering,' the training [that NGOs provided on rights for disadvantaged children] made [the children] either angry and destructive or frustrated and depressed. . . . [I]n everyday life, as one of the street working children ironically remarked, the issue is not whether poor people know themselves to have rights, but whether these are recognized by the people that matter."[40]

The Bangladesh case may in fact have deepened the practical and intellectual gulf between child rights advocates and more general human rights advocates, particularly activists concerned with labor rights. Scholar William Myers has argued that the Bangladesh case is a "real sore spot" in discussions between the two communities: labor rights advocates have "strongly supported it as a good example," while child rights activists have been "much more critical of it." As Myers explains:

> Child rights advocates insist that [children] should enjoy labor rights denied them by prevailing labor rights doctrines, and at least some child rights advocates charge that the current minimum age laws, the ILO, etc. deny children labor rights granted everyone by the *Universal Declaration of Human Rights* and other basic human rights instruments. . . . [T]here is no question in my mind that the case of Bangladesh has had an important role in forming the opinions of at least some of them.[41]

So discursively, this case has had significant impact, both in the emergence of the distinction between acceptable forms of child work and hazardous forms of child labor (the distinction at the heart of ILO Convention 182) and in the ensuing controversy surrounding it. The campaign has also influenced the more general emergence of the concept of child rights and succeeding controversies between and among child rights activists and more general human rights activists.

Intentional/Unintentional Consequences

The advocacy campaign waged transnationally against child labor in Bangladesh's garment industry fulfilled its original purpose of bringing this issue to the attention of business and government leaders in that country. An initial unintended consequence was the displacement of thousands of children from factories without income or schooling alternatives—which the campaign addressed by pressing for the creation of the MOU.

Susan Bissell, a former UNICEF–Bangladesh staff member working in Bangladesh at the time of the Harkin bill campaign, has argued that a longer-term, unintended consequence may have been the negative impact on the self-esteem of girls removed from factories.[42] She cites the work of Bangladeshi sociologist Nazli Kibria, whose research on female garment workers in Bangladesh has revealed that women have spoken "of their employment in positive terms, as an activity that had enhanced their sense of self-esteem and worth in the household." By extension, Bissell argues, girls working in the garment factories were likely to suffer a fall in self-esteem upon losing their jobs:

> [T]he implications of sudden retrenchment of girls from garment facto-
> ries were far-reaching for both economic and psycho-social reasons. . . .
> Many of the retrenched female workers were actually adolescent girls,
> for whom garment employment was the key to delayed age at marriage,
> to economic independence and to an increased role in decision making at
> a household level. This is not to ignore the value of education and the
> rights of these girls to participate in schools, but there are/were com-
> pelling reasons to learn more about the totality of their lives.[43]

Other authors have argued that the Harkin bill campaign and resulting MOU addressed the needs of only a small number of children in a high-profile sector (i.e., garments), while ignoring many others in more high-risk occupations—particularly in the informal sector. It had the unintended consequence of doing little to address the root causes of the child labor problem. Referring directly to the Bangladesh case, authors Ulrike Grote, Arnab Basu, and Diana Weinhol have argued: "If the underlying economic mechanisms compelling these children to work are not addressed, they will simply seek employment in the (by definition) unregulated informal sector, where jobs are generally more dangerous and lower paid, as regulation of the formal sector increases." The problem with many policy interventions, they continue, is that they "target the consequences of child labor, rather than its causes."[44]

Evaluating the Impact of the Mexico Campaigns

Analyzing the impact of transnational and domestic efforts to prevent pregnancy screening in the Mexican workplace is challenging. Academic and policy literature in English focuses exclusively on the U.S.-led campaign organized by Human Rights Watch around Submission 9701. It ignores the possible contribution of the 1998 national-level campaign. Indeed, other than work by this author, there is no scholarly literature in English on the campaign organized around the 1998 Tribunal on Reconciling Maternity and Work, and many U.S. scholars and activists appear unaware that this parallel campaign ever took place.[45]

Outside/Inside Dynamics: Impact on Targets

The targets of the HRW 9701 campaign included both the governments of Mexico and the United States, as well as the international corporations operating in the *maquiladora* zones. Early assessments of this campaign were fairly cautious. Lance Compa, an authority on the NAALC, wrote in 2001: "It is still too soon to know if a thorough change in policy and practice will take shape." As of late 1998, several firms cited in HRW reports had promised to stop pregnancy testing but "had not ended it entirely." But Compa also noted the overall impact of the case in elevating the profile of the issue within Mexico and internationally:

> [T]he NAALC complaint made an international affair of what had been a decades-long, hidden, entrenched, accepted practice in Mexico's burgeoning maquiladora sector. It set in motion a dynamic for changing the practice through new employer policies, proposed legislative changes, and escalated international attention if an evaluation committee of experts formed to address the case. The case and its attendant campaign efforts also elevated the visibility and influence of Mexican women's rights groups that had formerly been marginalized and ignored in their strictly domestic context.[46]

Other observers have expressed skepticism about the impact of the Human Rights Watch–led 9701 campaign on its targets. Even the one major concession the government of Mexico was ostensibly persuaded to make by the 9701 campaign—its admission in October 1998 that prehire pregnancy testing was discriminatory—is held in dispute: "Mexico may have recently conceded that in some instances pregnancy screening may be contrary to Mexican domestic law. Unfortunately, there is some disagreement over whether Mexico actually intended that statement or whether it was a misinterpretation."[47]

Lawyer Reka Koerner's assessment of the campaign's impact on corporate behavior is fairly typical: "While the submission process has brought pre-employment pregnancy discrimination into the public eye, Mexican maquiladoras will continue to discriminate against pregnant women unless the U.S. adopts a more aggressive stance."[48] Even corporations that shifted behavior in the wake of the 9701 campaign were not necessarily persuaded that the practice was illegal. General Motors and International Telephone and Telegraph, two companies cited in Human Rights Watch's reports on the case, both "maintained that their hiring practices were legal pursuant to Mexican law. ITT decided to discontinue the discriminatory hiring practices because the firm apparently considered the practices to be counter to the company morals, human rights ethics, and corporate culture. General Motors gave way, it seems, because of public concern expressed by non-governmental organizations that inundated the company with letters and phone calls."[49]

In 2003, the AFL-CIO's Solidarity Center produced a general assessment of worker rights in Mexico (compiled by Lance Compa), which includes an assessment of the 9701 campaign's impact. The book's general chapter on workplace discrimination opens with the pregnancy screening issue and deems it a "continuing blatant violation of workers' right to be free of discrimination in the workplace."[50] Neither the consultation process put in motion in response to the 9701 campaign nor related recommendations by other authorities seem to have had an impact on changing actual working conditions and labor rights in Mexico: "Mexico has failed to change the law where necessary and to effectively enforce the law where needed to put an end to widespread discrimination against women workers in the *maquiladora* factory zones."[51]

This pattern of neglect has persisted despite strong rhetoric on the issue from the Mexican government. Shortly after taking office in 2000, President Vincente Fox publicized his support for pregnant workers and vowed to stop pre-hire pregnancy testing.[52] Again, in July 2001, Fox publicly condemned employment-related pregnancy screening. His remarks generated considerable press coverage.[53]

Yet the government of Mexico has consistently ignored outside requests for updates and information on how it is concretely addressing the problem. The ILO, the U.S. State Department, and the Inter-American Commission on Human Rights have all referenced the problem in their own reporting and have recommended specific reforms. The ILO's Committee of Experts on the Application of Conventions and Recommendations (CEACR), the highest-level legal body responsible for examining compliance with ILO standards, has repeatedly prodded Mexico on the issue. In 2003, the CEACR requested that the government of Mexico "amend the Federal Labor Law to explicitly prohibit discrimination based on sex in recruitment and hiring for employment and in conditions of employment."[54] Seemingly in response, President Fox signed the Federal Law to Prevent and Eliminate Discrimination, which was approved unanimously by the Mexican Congress in April 2003, signed by the president on 9 June 2003, and officially published on 11 June 2003.[55] The law obliges federal authorities to strengthen antidiscrimination efforts "within their own agencies and in the public policy arenas where they have enforcement jurisdiction."[56] It calls for the creation of a "National Council for the Prevention of Discrimination," to draft corresponding regulations and establish penalties for workplace discrimination throughout the Mexican economy.

Yet the law is written in very general terms, and the council's enforcement capacity is not clearly spelled out. Many labor experts have predicted that the new law will have little effect on pregnancy screening because the practice is already prevented under existing Mexican labor law, yet is widespread because of lack of enforcement. Indeed, Eduardo Díaz, a Mexican labor rights advocate and lawyer, has argued that the new antidiscrimination law "does not go far enough. . . . Changes are needed in the Federal Labor Law."[57]

President Fox charged his labor secretary, Carlos Abascal, with leading efforts to reform Mexico's labor law, but the corresponding changes proposed in January 2003 to the Mexican Chamber of Deputies (the country's highest legislative body) have been met with widespread criticism at home and abroad. Scholar Linda Stevenson notes that "policy entrepreneurs" from two of the main opposition parties, the Partido Revolucionario Democrático (PRD) and the Partido Acción Nacional (PAN), had initially seemed poised to tackle the issue of discrimination against pregnant workers in 1998 and were "preparing to advocate for reforms in the Federal Labor Law." But over the next five years, the two parties "divided on their reform proposals," while the long dominant Partido Revolucionario Institucional (PRI) remained—in Stevenson's words— "not really interested in change." Hence, innovative proposals for strengthening the labor law's existing provisions on pregnancy screening never surfaced.[58]

As a result, the proposed labor law reforms—referred to as the "Abascal Project"[59]—do not include pregnancy screening explicitly among the forms of discrimination prohibited. (For example, proposed changes to article 3 include the addition of references to discrimination related to differential ability, opinions, social status, or "anything else that is against human dignity," but do not explicitly reference pregnancy.) In February 2005, Human Rights Watch issued a letter to key members of Mexico's Chamber of Deputies urging them not to approve the proposed reforms. While the letter concentrated principally on the detrimental effect the reforms would have on independent union organizing in the country, it also included a detailed critique of the Abascal Project's "failure to protect workers' right to freedom from sex discrimination"— specifically, its lack of concrete means to address the problem of workplace pregnancy screening.[60]

As HRW noted, a key goal of the 2004 National Human Rights Program put forward by President Fox was to "verify that pregnancy tests are not demanded of women wishing to access employment,"[61] but the

Abascal Project's proposed reforms would not come close to achieving this. Human Rights Watch's letter cited Mexico's inadequate response not only to the 1996 and 1998 reports published by HRW itself but also to a 1999 recommendation by the UN Committee on Economic, Social, and Cultural Rights that Mexico "adopt immediate steps towards the protection of women workers in the *maquiladoras*, including prohibiting the practice of demanding medical certification that prospective workers are not pregnant and taking legal action against employers who fail to comply."[62]

Preventing workplace pregnancy screening is therefore a problem at multiple levels. Within Mexico itself, there is widespread public cynicism related to the persistence of the problem, as evidenced in the interview findings included in this book. There are few to no publicly available data to demonstrate that Mexico's own national labor monitoring institutions are more effectively addressing the problem today than they were before the 9701 campaign—and data on pregnancy screening were scarce and hard to attain long before the campaign, and remain so.

The NAALC and other regional human rights instruments—as well as the ILO and UN treaty bodies such as the Committee on Economic, Social, and Cultural Rights—all appear to have been ineffective in persuading Mexico to take serious action on the pregnancy screening. As legal analyst Michelle Smith writes: "The process under NAALC is a slow one and it is unlikely that the submission will produce any substantial changes in the near future."[63] The 2003 AFL-CIO Solidarity Center report argues even more forcefully:

> The NAALC has failed to achieve its high purpose. Apparently more eager to maintain diplomatic niceties rather than tackle and solve worker rights violations, the three governments have demonstrated a lack of will to hold one another to their NAALC commitments. Some investigations and reports have led to significant findings and recommendations, but they have not produced change. Ministerial consultations have resulted only in research projects and tri-national conferences. Although these are often informative, they have not directly addressed or resolved worker rights violations documented and proven in NAALC proceedings.[64]

In a very mixed review, analyst Nicole Grimm writes that the U.S. National Administration Office for the side accord was "attentive" in its handling of the 9701 case—particularly in "its willingness to look beyond Mexican federal law to international law documents and non-legal Mexican sources for opinions about pre-hire pregnancy discrimination ... however, the lack of sanctions available under NAALC procedures for cases of gender discrimination may hinder truly effective enforcement of labor laws in the NAFTA free trades zones."[65]

The counterfactual argument—that the campaign *must* have had an impact on public policy and outcomes and the lives of women in the workplace (i.e., things would have been worse had the campaign not occurred)—is the one typically advanced by authors who argue that the 9701 campaign had an impact: "This submission, as well as the HRW investigation, received a tremendous amount of attention that *would likely not have been focused* on this issue otherwise. . . . Despite the harsh criticism NAALC has received for its inability to actually bind countries to any of its recommendations, NAALC is still an effective body in its persuasive powers" (emphasis added).[66]

Outside/Inside Dynamics: Impact on the Campaign Itself

The most overlooked aspect of the 9701 campaign is the fact that it gave rise both to the backdoor moves by activists along the border and to a parallel, secondary campaign crafted by Mexican feminist activists who sought to capitalize on the political space opened by international negotiations over Submission 9701. Both of these alternative ways of carrying out advocacy are overlooked in much of the literature on transnational advocacy related to pregnancy screening in Mexico.

Groups at the border used the resources and political space created by the transnational campaign to reinforce their already existing grassroots outreach on labor and economic rights. Feminist groups in Mexico City leveraged the uncomfortable position of the Mexican government amidst the 9701 negotiations to put forward proposals for domestic policy reform. The HRW campaign thus had a "second image reversed" effect on policy discourse in Mexico:[67] interstate relations over the 9701 campaign changed the nature of activity in the domestic political arena, giving local actors (both those at the border and feminist activists in Mexico City) new space and added leverage for engaging their own local constituencies—or, in the case of Mexico City–based feminists, space and leverage for engaging state representatives in discussions of institutional reform and policy implementation. Linda Stevenson offers one of the most nuanced and detailed analyses of how feminist political actors used the pregnancy screening issue to open new space for dialogue in Mexican politics, though she does not touch on the 1998 campaign on "reconciling maternity and work."[68]

An integrated discussion of the two campaigns not only highlights the effects of NAFTA on domestic policy, but also illuminates a new and original mechanism (i.e., the backdoor move) that helps explain transnational interaction in the Mexico case and beyond. While the HRW 9701 campaign may not have had significant practical impact either on the targets or in material terms, it did influence the evolution of organizing strategies among activists in Mexico, as both Stevenson's work and this book illustrate.

Material/Nonmaterial Aspects

The material impact of this campaign was admittedly limited. As discussed in chapter 4, the Mexican national teachers' union negotiated provisions banning pregnancy screening into its collective contract in 1999, and later that year Mexico City's mayor signed into force a local law prohibiting screening in that city. Stevenson notes, however, that public programs to assist women in Mexico City with pregnancy discrimination in the late 1990s were understaffed and underresourced, overwhelmed with complaints, and ultimately discontinued.[69]

The nonmaterial/discursive impact of the campaign was more significant. The 9701 campaign served as a catalyst for backdoor moves by Mexican NGOs that resulted in important local-level adaptations of the 9701 campaign's human rights frame—adaptations of Human Rights Watch's narrow civil and political rights frame to include economic rights dimensions (i.e., the right to work). Even more striking, feminist activists in Mexico City responded to the political opportunity presented in the form of the 9701 campaign by reconstructing the frame to suit broader social change objectives. They widened the existing frame (set by the 9701 campaign) considerably: they pointed out that women other than *maquila* workers were also affected by pregnancy screening (including women in white-collar public- and private-sector professions). They pointed out that women well beyond the border region were affected—indeed, women throughout the country faced the "tradeoff between maternity and work," as the title of their October 1998 tribunal aptly reflected. And they argued that real social change would not be achieved simply by halting the practice of pregnancy screening but instead must entail reconceptualizing the nature of work (to include social reproduction) and reenvisioning gender roles within the family and society.

These discursive changes never registered in the formal communications of the HRW 9701 campaign, where the focus remained on denouncing pregnancy screening in the maquiladoras as a violation of civil and political rights (i.e., the right to nondiscrimination in employment), as well as a violation of the reproductive right to choose the spacing and timing of children.[70] But Mexican activists nevertheless carried their additional messages forward at the local level, using an alternative set of human rights frames/messages.

Intentional/Unintentional Consequences

The intent of the 9701 campaign was to test the NAFTA labor side accord as a vehicle for international human rights advocacy and to bring the problem of pregnancy screening into public view in Mexico. Human Rights Watch and its Mexican counterpart NGOs found the North American Agreement on Labor Cooperation (NAALC) to be a cumbersome, time-consuming mechanism for advocacy, but they succeeded in raising public consciousness about the issue of pregnancy screening. Yet the practice persists.

Stevenson has included indicators on pregnancy screening policy within her broader analysis of the gendered dynamics of Mexican democratization. She has developed a three-part rating system to "assess the differing values of various policy actions" as follows:

- Rhetorical policy change: a policy proposal has "attained a minimal amount of social or political value by being mentioned in discourse by politicians or persons who brought it to the public's attention."
- Symbolic policy change: a policy proposal "has greater social or political benefit than simply to be used for political ends in public discourse . . . attains agenda status in a given legislature, is discussed and covered in the media, and/or is passed into law at that level . . . *does not yet necessarily generate material change or benefits*" (emphasis added).
- Material policy change: a policy proposal achieves " actual, tangible outcomes related to the implementation of the policy . . . measured by concrete changes."[71]

Stevenson ranks policy actions from lowest to highest impact (i.e., rhetorical is ranked lowest, material is ranked highest) and employs the ranking to assess seven policy actions taken by the Mexican government in response to contemporary feminist advocacy. These include actions taken in response to advocacy on "discrimination against pregnant workers." Stevenson argues that the actions taken in this issue area have been "symbolic"and therefore that "much . . . has yet to be implemented in ways that will result in material change . . . symbolic gains can serve as stepping stones for advocates to use to move toward more substantive changes."[72]

Beyond Mexico, the unintended ripple effect of the 9701 campaign has been significant—at least on a rhetorical level. References to pregnancy screening appear often in international analysis of human rights in Latin America and beyond. For example, United Nations treaty monitoring committees have flagged the issue not only to Mexico but also to other countries, including Croatia and Slovakia.[73] A 2000 edition of the North American Congress on Latin America's *NACLA Report on the Americas* included seventeen articles from leading human rights analysts and activists region-wide, two of which referenced pregnancy screening directly (one in relation to Mexico and another in relation to Chile).[74] And corporate codes of conduct developed by businesses worldwide routinely include prohibitions on pregnancy screening.[75] But in all of these instances, the problem is generally presented as one of discrimination—despite efforts to widen the human rights frame on the part of both activists on the Mexican border and feminists in the 1998 Mexico City–based campaign.

Concluding Note

Jonathan Fox's three-part framework for impact analysis offers a lens through which to analyze not only the concrete effects of the Bangladesh and Mexico campaigns on policy outcomes in those countries, but also the role that blocking and backdoor moves played, respectively, in shaping normative understandings within these campaigns and beyond. By assessing impact on three levels—in terms of "outside/inside" dynamics, material/nonmaterial aspects, and intentional/unintentional consequences—this chapter has sought to provide a comprehensive view of norms evolution in the context of these two campaigns, as well as a template for future study of the dynamics of transnational advocacy over time.

Conclusion

Hundreds of thousands of people in countries around the world marshaled campaigns in defense of workers' rights and social justice in the 1990s. This book further develops the transnational advocacy story by parsing campaigns into sending and receiving ends, by opening the possibility of more than "boomerang" campaign emergence, and by introducing blocking and backdoor moves as mechanisms central to campaign evolution. These mechanisms increase the dynamism and complexity of interaction among domestic political forces (such as social movements, local political actors, or business lobbies) and international ones (such as multilateral organizations, regional trade institutions, and transnational advocacy networks). They also enrich the causal explanation of norms evolution, adding complexity to the norms emergence stage.

Blocking and backdoor moves shed light on the role that actors other than norms entrepreneurs play as generators of new normative understandings and as catalysts for policy change. Differences among members of networks matter—not only in terms of access to political power, media, and resources (as Clifford Bob has shown),[1] but also in terms of fundamental understandings of human rights, as this book demonstrates. Who sets the rights agenda of a campaign may change as a result of blocking and backdoor moves. By employing such moves, less powerful actors within networks can challenge the dominant interpretation of norms in a given campaign. In doing so, they increase their chances of transforming the rights at stake and of influencing policy outcomes.

Activists block and make backdoor moves for principled as well as material reasons. They are often as concerned about the economic impact an advocacy campaign could have on their well-being as they are about the norms at stake—particularly when campaigns around labor rights, for example, threaten consumer boycotts or use other types of economic leverage as tools of influence. A number of factors affect the decision to block or make backdoor moves, including the form in which a campaign evolves; the presence or absence of economic sanctions; and the presence or absence of shared interests.

Whereas Keck and Sikkink's boomerang form of campaign evolution assumes a relative degree of concord within a transnational advocacy network, the "outside-in" and "dual-target" forms of campaign evolution identified in this book highlight the presence of differences and, in some cases, outright conflict among activists. Outside-in campaigns, for example, are frequently launched without consultation between sending- and receiving-end activists, increasing the likelihood that blocking will occur on the part of those who receive the full force of a campaign out of sync with their local understandings of norms and their own priorities for action. The effect of either blocking or backdoor moves may be to widen the normative understandings in a campaign—but widening is not automatic. In the case studies analyzed here, blocking led to more significant shifts in normative understandings than did backdoor moves.

This book has explored the dynamic area of economic and labor rights theory, policy advocacy, and activism—a new frontier in the human rights field. The institutions discussed in the book are pioneering and innovative: The NAFTA side accord on labor was the first trade agreement of its kind to include mechanisms for labor rights protection and promotion. The memorandum of understanding on child labor brokered between business, government, and UN organizations in Bangladesh was also a first. Yet as each of the case studies shows, more remarkable than the creation of these institutions themselves was how activists within countries and across borders used the political space opened by these institutions to advance multiple normative agendas.

In both Bangladesh and Mexico, the campaigns discussed did more than simply challenge state or corporate power. They opened an intense debate at the national, regional, and international level over the meaning of child labor, in the one case, and the relationship between discrimination, work, and reproduction, in the other. As these case studies illustrate, activists themselves engaged in contestation with one another—

both directly and indirectly—over the nature and scope of the rights to be protected. They did so by employing blocking and backdoor moves.

Do the concepts introduced in the book travel beyond these two cases? Do they help advance broader theorizing? Consider the following examples. The Jubilee 2000 debt relief movement emerged in the mid-1990s with the aim of reducing the debt burden of the poorest countries through debt forgiveness timed to coincide with the turn of the millennium. The name "Jubilee" was drawn from the biblical reference in Leviticus 25 to periodic debt forgiveness in Jewish tradition—a "jubilee" year. Activists in the movement seized on the World Bank and International Monetary Fund's identification in 1996 of forty countries in Africa, Latin America, and Asia as "heavily indebted poor countries" (HIPC) and pushed thereafter for coordinated bilateral and multilateral debt forgiveness by the year 2000. They also called for corresponding reinvestment in basic human development priorities by debtors and international donors. Popular icons such as the rock star Bono championed the campaign, adding to its public support and media attention.[2]

However, the Jubilee movement split into "Jubilee South" and "Jubilee North" in 1999. Jubilee South is principally made up of groups based in developing countries. Its members have entirely rejected the notion of developing country debt, insisting instead that industrialized countries owe the South for the wealth the North has expropriated from the region historically. These citizens reject their own governments' participation in debt reduction negotiations; their slogan is "Don't Owe! Won't Pay!" Jubilee North, by contrast, was willing to support debt forgiveness negotiations under the existing terms of the HIPC initiative. Jubilee South could thus be argued to have blocked the debt relief movement. Jubilee North has made backdoor moves within the scope of broader, official debt relief negotiations.[3]

A second example centers on the activities of African American women in the U.S. civil rights movement, which could be interpreted in terms of backdoor moves. Although this movement was domestic rather than transnational, the power relations and corresponding interactions among movement actors are similar in key respects to those in the case studies developed in this book. African American men have traditionally been considered the public face of the American civil rights movement. Individual women may have played prominent roles in the movement, such as Rosa Parks. Her refusal to abide by rules for segregated seating on a public bus in 1955 sparked the Montgomery, Alabama, bus boycott, a galvanizing event for the movement.[4] But historians, social commentators, and the public alike have typically underplayed the strategic importance of African American women's achievements and influence, if not neglected them entirely, because they have not looked for actors using backdoor moves.

New scholarship argues that African American women played multiple and diverse roles in the American civil rights movement, and that the movement as a whole must be reinterpreted in terms of multilayered leadership and corresponding class, race, and gender dynamics.[5] Female and male activists in the movement clearly had shared interests in seeing the movement succeed. But women had their own aims as well as corresponding strategies for achieving them. Moreover, African American women involved in the civil rights movement were not uniform in their experiences, interests, or goals. Backdoor moves would thus have been one tool female activists could have employed to achieve their varying aims, without derailing the movement as a whole.

Jubilee 2000, the American civil rights movement, and the cases developed in this book illustrate that those targeted by a campaign—representatives of government, business, or other powerful institutions in society—can improve their odds for successfully negotiating with activists if they understand the rights at stake. A World Bank representative negotiating with representatives of Jubilee South, for example, could predict that the scope of bargaining would *not* occur within the HIPC framework if she were aware of the multiple currents within the movement.

The same is true for members of advocacy networks themselves. Conflicting understandings of rights within a single network heighten the risk of collective action failures. Acknowledging and understanding such differences are critical to developing shared strategies for effective, inclusive advocacy—and meaningful solutions to the problems that provoked contentious politics in the first place. Feminist activists in Mexico City, for example, risked losing the support of female labor rights activists from the Mexican border when they failed to consult them in the early stages of planning the national Tribunal on Reconciling Maternity and Work. Only after careful fence-mending did some of the border-based activists agree to come to Mexico City for the tribunal, where they offered firsthand testimony on conditions in the maquiladoras and surrounding communities—a vital element of this larger event.

On the practical side, digging beneath the official narrative of a campaign reveals new insights into how normative understandings evolve and how policy outcomes may (or may not) change as a result of conflicts within networks. It unpacks the "mutual transformation" that takes place among activists, signaled in earlier work on transnational advocacy.[6] But the question remains: does this transformation extend beyond campaign participants to the larger population the campaigns intended to influence or assist? Do blocking and backdoor moves help translate norms into policy action?

The impact of both the Bangladesh and Mexico campaigns is still debated. In Bangladesh, the novel memorandum of understanding created to prevent child labor in the garment industry did include funds for assisting displaced child workers with stipends and schooling. And several years after the Bangladesh campaign ended, ILO member states adopted a convention on the worst forms of child labor that reflected subtler distinctions in the definition of child labor than had earlier conventions. The creation of this new convention resulted, in part, from the normative tumult central to the Bangladesh campaign. Yet there are still questions over what happened to tens of thousands of children dismissed from factories *before* the agreement was signed, and there is skepticism over whether or not children at greatest risk are being protected in Bangladesh or elsewhere.

In Mexico, despite nearly four years of investigation, campaigning, and even presidential consultations on the issue of workplace pregnancy screening, many women remain unaware that the practice is a violation of their rights. It continues, albeit better hidden than before the campaign began. Mexican feminists' far-reaching goal of reconciling maternity and work, along with corresponding changes in social norms and public policy, seems even farther out of reach in an increasingly harsh national and regional labor environment. At the national level in Mexico and in many other countries, agencies tasked with promoting labor rights, social development, and trade policy rarely collaborate on domestic or international policymaking. There is little shared understanding of how labor and economic rights—the focus of the campaigns discussed here—relate to human rights more generally.

Regardless of locale, domestic and international institutions are largely unprepared to accommodate these and other new types of human rights claim making. The ILO, which is tasked with protecting and promoting labor rights globally, is well positioned to do so. However, it operates separately from other human rights institutions and has only begun, under new leadership, to bridge the divides among different types of rights in policy and program efforts.

Given the institutional, political, and other constraints outlined, does it make more sense to concentrate on promoting a narrow human rights agenda focused on civil and political rights, the mainstay of traditional human rights advocacy? Or should activists use blocking and/or backdoor moves to advance new rights claims that bridge the divides between civil, political, economic, and social rights? In the Mexico case, staff of Human Rights Watch clearly believed that focusing on the civil and political rights dimensions of pregnancy discrimination was most practical—and did so. Grassroots groups in both Mexico and Bangladesh, however, pushed for a broader framing of human rights. Whether they succeeded in changing rights discourse and corresponding policy action is less central to this book than why and how they *intended* to do so.

The dogged determinism of activists in these cases to make their claims heard—directly or indirectly—is a force to be reckoned with, a form of unexpected power that stands to transform not only our academic understanding of contentious politics, but also politics on the ground. Further research could help specify with greater precision the conditions under which the mechanisms introduced here occur. It would be useful to identify a wide range of both "outside-in" and "dual-target" campaigns and to explore whether the proposed relationship between these types of campaign evolution and blocking and backdoor moves, respectively, holds over a broader range of cases. Similarly, one could develop a large sample of campaigns in which economic sanctions were threatened (e.g., consumer boycotts, trade sanctions, and so on) and test whether or not these consistently predispose receiving-end activists to block.

It would also be useful to develop a succinct, replicable set of criteria for "shared interests" and to compile a wider set of cases through which to explore systematically the relationship between such interests and the likelihood of backdoor moves. A final research challenge would be to analyze in greater depth and on multiple levels the impact of these mechanisms on campaigns themselves and on broader policy outcomes. Jonathan Fox's three contrasting pairs of concepts provide a starting point here, but there are no doubt other frameworks for evaluation that could be developed and applied.

All of these research challenges are beyond the scope of this book. The ideas introduced here pave the way for new theory building. They can also be used by activists in the field in their struggles for workers' rights, economic justice, and other issues that straddle the artificial intellectual divides so often imposed in theory on human rights.

Appendix I
Questionnaire—Bangladesh Interviews

NAME and TITLE(S) OF RESPONDENT:
INSTITUTIONAL AFFILIATION:
Telephone(s):
Fax:
Address:

1) Do you know about the campaign against child labor in Bangladesh, related to the Harkin Bill in the mid-1990s?
2) How did you learn about it?
3) Did you or your organization take part in the campaign—or did you oppose it?
4) Why did you (or your organization) take part in the campaign—or not?
5) Do you think that the majority of individuals or organizations involved in the campaign were from: a) industrialized countries; b) developing countries; c) some combination?
6) What specifically did you do in relation to the campaign?

   Possible answers:
   a) grassroots education or service work (Please give examples.)
   b) information exchange with other organizations (Please give examples.)

In Bangladesh? Y/N
In industrialized countries? Y/N
In developing countries? Y/N

c) lobbying to influence key decision-makers (Please give examples.)
In Bangladesh? Y/N
In industrialized countries? Y/N
In developing countries? Y/N

7) Did you consider your participation in the campaign, or your opposition to it: a) an extension of your regular activity, OR b) something new?

8) How do you characterize the campaign?
Possible answers: a) as a campaign about human rights; b) about labor rights; c) about children's rights? How do you distinguish between these types of rights, if at all?

9) What were the positive and negative aspects of the campaign?

10) Rank the impact of the campaign on the following relationships:
[0 = None; 1 = Low impact; 2 = Medium impact; 3 = High impact]

A. **Relations among Bangladeshi NGOs and:**
NGOs in other countries [   ]
Government of Bangladesh [   ]
Other governments [   ]
Unions in Bangladesh [   ]
Unions in other countries [   ]

B. **Relations among Bangladeshi companies and:**
Companies in other countries [   ]
Government of Bangladesh [   ]
Other governments [   ]
Unions in Bangladesh [   ]
Unions in other countries [   ]
NGOs in Bangladesh [   ]
NGOs in other countries [   ]

C. **Relations between the Government of Bangladesh and:**
Other governments [   ]
UN organizations [   ]

D. **Relations between UN organizations and:**
NGOs in Bangladesh [   ]
Unions in Bangladesh [   ]
Companies in Bangladesh [   ]

11) Were you (or your organization) involved in similar campaigns in the 1990s? Which ones? How do they relate, if at all, to your participation in (or opposition to) the child labor campaign?

12) Was the child labor campaign part of a broader movement? If so, what would you call that movement?
Possible answers: a) anti-free trade; b) anti-globalization; c) anti-corporate; d) pro-social justice; e) pro-human rights; f) pro-labor rights; g) pro-economic rights; h) other?

Appendix 2
Questionnaire—Mexico Interviews

1) ¿Sabe usted sobre una campaña contra exámenes de embarazo en las maquiladoras?

2) ¿Cómo aprendió de la campaña?

3) Si participó usted, ¿cómo lo hizo? ¿Cuáles fueron sus propias actividades o las de su organización?

4) ¿Por qué decidió (o decidieron) de participar?

5) ¿Considera usted su participación en la campaña (si hubo): a) una extensión de su actividad normal; b) o fue algo nuevo?

6) ¿Cuáles fueron las ventajas y/o desventajas de participar?

7) ¿Piensa usted que la campaña tenía un impacto en la situación actual de la mujer en la maquila—sí o no, y por qué?

8) ¿Cómo caracteriza la campaña: a) una campaña sobre derechos humanos; b) sobre derechos laborales; c) sobre derechos de la mujer? ¿Distingue usted entre esos derechos? Si lo hace, ¿cómo explica las diferencias?

9) ¿Considera usted esta campaña parte de un movimiento más amplio? Si es cierto, ¿cómo caracteriza tal movimiento?

10) ¿Piensa usted que esta campaña sobre exámenes de embarazo tiene algo que ver con las manifestaciones contra el WTO? ¿Sí o no, y por qué?

11) ¿Hay otras(os) colegas quienes llevaron un rol en la campana "9701" (o tienen una opinión sobre cosas relacionadas a mi investigación) con quienes debo hablar?

Appendix 3
Overview of Normative References for Activism on Pregnancy Screening

Ley Federal del Trabajo (Mexican Labor Law)[1]

Article 3: prohibits discrimination based on race, sex, religion, political doctrine or social condition; stipulates preference in hiring for sole source of household income.

Article 4: prohibits discrimination based on race, sex, age, religion, political doctrine, or social condition.

Article 47: stipulates grounds for firing and related responsibilities of employers.

Article 50: outlines rights related to severance compensation.

Article 133, Sections 1 and 7: also prohibit discrimination, for reasons of age or sex.

Articles 154 and 156: stipulate rights of hiring preference, seniority, and promotion.

Articles 164–72: outline specific protections for working mothers, aimed at avoiding "endangering the worker or the product of her pregnancy."

Constitution of Mexico[2]

Article 4 (1974): establishes formal juridical equality between women and men, along with the right of "all people to decide in a free, responsible, and informed manner on the number and spacing of children" and the right to "protection of health."

Article 5: stipulates that "no person can be legally impeded from dedicating him/herself to a profession, industry, or job that suits him/her."

Article 123: stipulates that all people have the "right to work that is dignified and socially useful." This includes provisions for pregnant workers to have a total of three months off (six weeks prior to delivery, six weeks afterward). During this time, they will receive full salary, with the guarantee of the same position upon return.

ILO Conventions[3]

Convention 111 (1958), Discrimination in Employment and Occupation

Convention 158, Termination of Employment (1982)

Recommendation 12 (1921), Maternity Protection (Agriculture) Recommendation

Recommendation 95 (1952), Maternity Protection Recommendation

UN Treaties and Conference Declarations[4]

International Covenant on Civil and Political Rights

Convention on Elimination of All Forms of Discrimination against Women (CEDAW), Article 11, 1(b) and 2(a): right to equality in hiring and prohibition on discrimination in employment, including for reasons of pregnancy.

International Conference on Population and Development (Cairo, 1994): called for the elimination of "discriminatory practices by employers against women, such as requiring tests for contraceptive use or statements about pregnancy."

World Summit on Social Development (Copenhagen, 1995), Declaration and Programme of Action

Fourth World Conference on Women (Beijing, 1995), Declaration and Platform for Action

Other

American Convention on Human Rights

North American Agreement on Labor Cooperation

Notes

1. New Dynamics in Transnational Advocacy

1. Margaret Keck and Kathryn Sikkink, *Activists Beyond Borders: Transnational Advocacy Networks in International Politics* (Ithaca: Cornell University Press, 1998). See also Keck and Sikkink, "Transnational Advocacy Networks in International and Regional Politics," *International Social Science Journal* 159 (1999): 89–101; and Keck and Sikkink, "Transnational Advocacy Networks in Movement Society," in *The Social Movement Society: Contentious Politics for a New Century,* ed. David S. Meyer and Sidney Tarrow (Lanham, MD: Rowman and Littlefield, 1998), 217–62. These authors define campaigns as "sets of strategically linked activities in which members of diffuse principled networks develop explicit, visible ties and mutually recognized roles toward a common goal (generally a common target)." "Transnational Advocacy Networks in Movement Society," 228.

2. A norm is a standard of behavior defined in terms of rights and obligations, which incorporates collective expectations for the appropriate behavior of actors with a given identity. Stephen D. Krasner, "Structural Causes and Regime Consequences: Regimes as Intervening Variables," in *International Regimes,* ed. Krasner (Ithaca: Cornell University Press, 1983), 2. Peter J. Katzenstein, ed., *The Culture of National Security: Norms and Identity in World Politics* (New York: Columbia University Press, 1996), 5.

3. Martha Finnemore and Kathryn Sikkink map a multistage process that moves from emergence to tipping point to norms cascade and subsequent internalization, in "International Norm Dynamics and Political Change," *International Organization* 52, no. 4 (autumn 1998): 887–917.

4. Mayer Zald, "Culture, Ideology, and Strategic Framing," in *Comparative Perspectives on Social Movements,* ed. Doug McAdam, John D. McCarthy, and Zald (Cambridge: Cambridge University Press, 1996), 262. Zald defines framing as the use of "specific metaphors, symbolic representations, and cognitive cues" to name wrongs and propose or demand remedies.

5. Keck and Sikkink, "Transnational Advocacy Networks in International and

Regional Politics," 92, 100. See also Keck and Sikkink, *Activists Beyond Borders*, 211, 214–16.

6. Clifford Bob explores similar issues in "Constructing New Human Rights Norms: A Theoretical Framework," paper presented at the annual meeting of the International Studies Association, Montreal, Canada, 17–20 March 2004.

7. Albert S. Yee, "The Causal Effects of Ideas on Policies," *International Organization* 50, no. 1 (winter 1996): 68–108.

8. John Gerring, *Case Study Research: Principles and Practices* (Cambridge: Cambridge University Press, forthcoming).

9. United Nations Development Programme, *Human Development Report 1995* (New York: Oxford University Press, 1995).

10. Activism on labor and economic rights is by no means a wholly new phenomenon. For historical references, see Keck and Sikkink, *Activists Beyond Borders*, 41–51; Andrew Ross, introduction, in *No Sweat: Fashion, Free Trade and the Rights of Garment Workers*, ed. Ross (London: Verso, 1997), 10–18; Upendra Baxi, "The Development of the Right to Development," in *Human Rights: New Dimensions and Challenges*, ed. Janusz Symonides (Brookfield, MA: Ashgate, 1998), 99–116.

11. Jon Elster, *Alchemies of the Mind: Rationality and the Emotions* (Cambridge: Cambridget University Press, 1999), 24, 26.

12. Doug McAdam, Sidney Tarrow, and Charles Tilly, *Dynamics of Contention* (Cambridge: Cambridge University Press, 2001), 24–26.

13. Yee, "Causal Effects of Ideas on Policies," 82–85.

14. Doug McAdam, Sidney Tarrow, and Charles Tilly, "Toward an Integrated Perspective on Social Movements and Revolution," in *Comparative Politics: Rationality, Culture and Structure*, ed. Mark I. Lichback and Alan S. Zuckerman (Cambridge: Cambridge University Press, 1997), 143; Marco Giugni, *How Social Movements Matter* (Minneapolis: University of Minnesota Press, 1999); and Sidney Tarrow, *Power in Movement: Social Movements and Contentious Politics*, 2nd ed. (Cambridge: Cambridge University Press, 1998).

15. Keck and Sikkink, *Activists Beyond Borders*, 12–13.

16. Finnemore and Sikkink, "International Norm Dynamics," 898.

17. James C. Scott's discussion of passive resistance in *Domination and the Arts of Resistance: Hidden Transcripts* (New Haven: Yale University Press, 1990) offers insight into bottom-up mechanisms similar to those introduced in this book, but blocking and backdoor moves are active, rather than passive.

18. Miguel Carter, "Ideal Interest Mobilization: Explaining the Formation of Brazil's Landless Social Movement" (Ph.D. diss., Columbia University, 2002), 4.

19. Beth Stephens explores various legal approaches for preventing abuse of basic civil and political rights by international corporations in her articles "Corporate Liability: Enforcing Human Rights through Domestic Litigation," *Hastings International and Comparative Law Review* 24, no. 3 (spring 2001): 401–13, and "The Amorality of Profit: Transnational Corporations and Human Rights," *Berkeley Journal of International Law* 20, no. 1 (2002): 45–90.

20. For an exception, see Charles Tilly's database of contentious events compiled for *Popular Contention in Great Britain, 1758–1834* (Cambridge: Harvard University Press, 1995), reviewed by Sidney Tarrow, "Social Movements in Contentious Politics: A Review Essay," *American Political Science Review* 90, no. 4 (December 1996): 874–83.

21. Gerring, *Case Study Research*.

22. Keck and Sikkink, *Activists Beyond Borders*, 12.

23. Philip Alston, "The Commission on Human Rights," in *The United Nations and Human Rights: A Critical Appraisal*, ed. Alston (Oxford: Clarendon Press, 1992), 188, 191. Maria Green, "What We Talk About When We Talk About Indicators: Current Approaches to Human Rights Measurement," *Human Rights Quarterly* 23 (2001): 1062–97. Paul Hunt, *Reclaiming Social Rights: International and Comparative Perspectives* (Brookfield,

VT: Dartmouth Publishing Group, 1996). Rolf Kunnemann, "A Coherent Approach to Human Rights," *Human Rights Quarterly* 17, no. 2 (1995): 323–42. Shareen Hertel, "Why Bother? Measuring Economic Rights—The Research Agenda," *International Studies Perspectives* 7, no. 3 (forthcoming).

24. Full text of the International Covenant on Economic, Social and Cultural Rights is available electronically via http://www.ohchr.org/english/law/cescr.htm.

25. Lance Compa, "The Promise and Perils of 'Core' Labor Rights in Global Trade and Investment," paper presented at the Human Rights for the Twenty-First Century conference, The Graduate Center, City University of New York, New York City, 17–18 November 2000. Christopher Candland, "How Do International Norms Evolve? Debate and Action on International Labor Standards," paper presented at the annual meeting of the American Political Science Association, Washington, DC, 28–31 August 1997. Brian Burgoon, "Uncertain Coalitions and the Political Economy of Fair Trade: Labor Rights Linkage in Domestic and International Politics," paper presented at the annual meeting of the International Studies Association, Chicago, IL, 20–24 February 2001.

26. Jackie Smith, "Transnational Political Processes and the Human Rights Movement," *Research in Social Movements, Conflicts and Change* 18 (1995): 185–219. Jackie Smith, "Globalizing Resistance: The Battle of Seattle and the Future of Social Movements," *Mobilization* 6, no. 1 (spring 2001): 1–19. Shareen Hertel, "What Was All the Shouting About? Strategic bargaining and protest at the WTO Third Ministerial (Seattle, Washington USA—November 1999)," *Human Rights Review* 6, no. 3 (April–June 2005): 102–18.

27. Peter Evans, "Fighting Marginalization with Transnational Networks: Counter-Hegemonic Globalization," *Contemporary Sociology* 29, no. 1 (January 2000): 230–41. Ann Marie Clark, Elisabeth J. Friedman, and Kathryn Hochstetler, "The Sovereign Limits of Global Civil Society: A Comparison of NGO Participation in UN World Conferences on the Environment, Human Rights, and Women," *World Politics* 51, no. 1 (October 1988): 1–25. Jonathan Fox, "Assessing Binational Civil Society Coalitions: Lessons from the US-Mexico Experience," working paper no. 26, University of California–Santa Cruz, April 2000. Heather Williams, "Mobile Capital and Transborder Labor Rights Mobilization," *Politics and Society* 27, no. 1 (March 1999): 139–66.

28. Ann M. Florini, ed., *The Third Force: The Rise of Transnational Civil Society* (Washington, DC: Brookings Institution Press, 2000). Michael Edwards and John Gaventa, eds., *Global Citizen Action* (Boulder, CO: Lynne Rienner, 2001).

29. Clark, Friedman, and Hochstetler highlight differing notions of human rights among groups involved in transnational activism in "Sovereign Limits," 29, 30, 32.

30. Finnemore and Sikkink, "International Norm Dynamics," 891–93, review related debates.

31. Paul Kowert and Jeffrey Legro, "Norms, Identity and Their Limits: A Theoretical Reprise," in *The Culture of National Security: Norms and Identity in World Politics*, ed. Peter J. Katzenstein (New York: Columbia University Press, 1996), 451–97, especially p. 454.

32. McAdam, Tarrow, and Tilly, *Dynamics of Contention*.

33. Stephen Van Evera, *Guide to Methods for Students of Political Science* (Ithaca: Cornell University Press, 1997), 77.

34. Van Evera, *Guide to Methods*; Alexander George and Tim McKeown, "Case Studies and Theories of Organizational Decisionmaking," *Advances in International Information Processing* 2 (1985): 21–58. See also Gerring, *Case Study Research*.

2. Conflict and Change within Advocacy Networks

1. Martha Finnemore and Kathryn Sikkink, "International Norm Dynamics and Political Change," *International Organization* 52, no. 4 (autumn 1998): 898.

2. Paul Kowert and Jeffrey Legro, "Norms, Identity and Their Limits," in *The Culture of National Security: Norms and Identity in World Politics,* ed. Peter J. Katzenstein (New York: Columbia University Press, 1996), 451–97, especially pp. 469–470.

3. Finnemore and Sikkink, "International Norm Dynamics," 887–917.

4. Clifford Bob, "Constructing New Human Rights Norms: A Theoretical Framework," paper presented at the annual meeting of the International Studies Association, Montreal, Canada, 17–20 March 2004, 3.

5. Ibid., 5.

6. Ibid., 9.

7. Ibid.

8. Mayer Zald, "Culture, Ideology, and Strategic Framing," in *Comparative Perspectives on Social Movements,* ed. Doug McAdam, John D. McCarthy, and Zald (Cambridge: Cambridge University Press, 1996), 261–74.

9. Kowert and Legro, "Norms, Identity and Their Limits," 494. Anthony Giddens, *The Constitution of Society: Outline of the Theory of Structuration* (Cambridge: Cambridge University Press, 1984). Giddens, *New Rules of Sociological Method: A Positive Critique of Interpretative Sociologies* (Stanford: Stanford University Press, 1993).

10. United Nations, "Annotations on the Text of the Draft International Covenants on Human Rights," UN Doc. A/2929 (1955), 7, cited in Henry J. Steiner and Philip Alston, "Economic and Social Rights," in *International Human Rights in Context: Law, Politics and Morals,* ed. Steiner and Alston (Oxford: Clarendon Press, 1996), 261.

11. Ida Koch, "Social Rights as Components in the Civil Right to Personal Liberty: Another Step Forward in the Integrated Human Rights Approach?" *Netherlands Quarterly of Human Rights* 20, no. 1 (2002): 29–51.

12. For example, the World Trade Organization's Third Ministerial Meeting at Seattle in November 1999 was riven by debates over labor standards linkage. While U.S.-based groups such as the Center of Concern or Friends of the Earth lobbied hard for linkages, developing country-based activists such as Malaysian Martin Khor warned against attaching new "conditionalities" that would "tie the WTO system in knots." Shareen Hertel, "What Was All the Shouting About? Strategic Bargaining and Protest at the WTO Third Ministerial (Seattle, Washington, USA—November 1999), *Human Rights Review* 6, no. 3 (April–June 2005): 111. Mark Anner, "The International Trade Union Campaign for Core Labor Standards in the WTO," *Working USA* 5, no. 1 (summer 2001): 43–63.

13. Finnemore and Sikkink, "International Norm Dynamics," 897.

14. Virginia Leary, "The Paradox of Workers' Rights as Human Rights," in *Human Rights, Labor Rights, and International Trade,* ed. Lance Compa and Stephen Diamond (Philadelphia: University of Pennsylvania Press, 1996), 22–47.

15. The constitutions of both Mexico and Bangladesh include references to the right to work. See articles 5 and 123 of the Mexican Constitution, available electronically via http://www.cddhcu.gob.mx/leyinfo/. The Constitution of the People's Republic of Bangladesh includes several references, among them part II, 15 (b) and 20 (1). The latter stipulates that "work is a right, a duty and a matter of honour for every citizen." Full text is available electronically via http://www.pmo.gov.bd/constitution/index.htm

16. Article 23, subsection 3, of the Universal Declaration of Human Rights references the right to a "just and favourable remuneration ensuring for himself and his family, an existence worthy of human dignity, and supplemented, if necessary, by other means of social protection."

17. Shareen Hertel, "Why Bother? Measuring Economic Rights—The Research Agenda," *International Studies Perspectives* 7, no. 3 (forthcoming). Clair Apodaca, "Measuring Women's Economic and Social Rights Achievement," *Human Rights Quarterly* 20, no. 1 (1998): 139–72. Audrey R. Chapman, "A 'Violations Approach' for Monitoring the

International Covenant on Economic, Social and Cultural Rights," *Human Rights Quarterly* 18, no. 1 (1996): 23–66.

18. Philip Alston, "The Commission on Human Rights," in *The United Nations and Human Rights: A Critical Appraisal* ed. Alston (Oxford: Clarendon Press, 1992). Leilani Farha, "Women's Rights and Economics: How Can We Promote Women's Economic, Social and Cultural Rights Internationally?" *AWID News* 4, no. 3 (autumn 2000): 1.

19. Virginia Leary, "Lessons from the Experience of the International Labour Organisation," in Alston, *United Nations and Human Rights*, 580–619.

20. Margaret Keck and Kathryn Sikkink, "Transnational Advocacy Networks in Movement Society," in *The Social Movement Society: Contentious Politics for a New Century*, ed. David S. Meyer and Sidney Tarrow (Lanham, MD: Rowman and Littlefield, 1998), 228.

21. Sidney Tarrow, "From Lumping to Splitting: Specifying Globalization and Resistance," in *Globalization and Resistance: Transnational Dimensions of Social Movements*, ed. Jackie Smith and Hank Johnston (Lanham, MD: Rowman and Littlefield, 2002), 236.

22. Examples include Thomas Risse, Stephen C. Ropp, and Kathryn Sikkink, *The Power of Human Rights: International Norms and Domestic Change* (Cambridge: Cambridge University Press, 1999); Katzenstein, *Culture of National Security*; Audie Klotz, *Norms in International Relations: The Struggle against Apartheid* (Ithaca: Cornell University Press, 1995).

23. John Cassidy, "Master of Disaster," *New Yorker*, 15 July 2002, 82–86. Joseph Stiglitz, *Globalization and Its Discontents* (New York: Norton, 2002). George Soros, *On Globalization* (New York: Public Affairs, 2002).

24. James Mahoney, "Beyond Correlational Analysis: Recent Innovations in Theory and Method," *Sociological Forum* 16, no. 3 (September 2001): 575–93, especially pp. 579–80.

25. Jon Elster has defined mechanisms as "frequently occurring and easily recognizable causal patterns that are triggered under generally unknown conditions or with indeterminate consequences . . . which allow us to explain, but not predict." *Alchemies of the Mind: Rationality and the Emotions* (Cambridge: Cambridge University Press, 1999), 1.

26. Albert S. Yee, "The Causal Effects of Ideas on Policies," *International Organization* 50, no. 1 (winter 1996): 69–108, especially pp. 82–85. Arthur Stinchcombe, "The conditions of fruitfulness of theorizing about mechanisms in social science," in *Social Theory and Social Policy: Essays in Honor of James S. Coleman*, ed. Aage B. Sorensen and Seymour Spilerman (Westport, CT: Praeger 1993), 24, 25.

27. Doug McAdam, Sidney Tarrow, and Charles Tilly, *Dynamics of Contention* (Cambridge: Cambridge University Press, 2001), 24–26.

28. Ibid., 85, 310.

29. Finnemore and Sikkink, "International Norm Dynamics," 904–5

30. Margaret Keck and Kathryn Sikkink, *Activists Beyond Borders: Transnational Advocacy Networks in International Politics* (Ithaca: Cornell University Press, 1998), 12–13.

31. Jill Gabrielle Klein, Craig N. Smith, and Andrew John, "Why We Boycott: Consumer Motivations for Boycott Participation," *Journal of Marketing* 68, no. 3 (2003): 92–110. Monroe Friedman, "Grassroots Groups Confront the Corporation: Contemporary Strategies in Historical Perspective," *Journal of Social Issues* 52, no. 1 (spring 1996): 153–68. Michael E. Nielsen, "The Politics of Corporate Responsibility and Child Labour in the Bangladeshi Garment Industry," *International Affairs* 81, no. 3 (May 2005): 559–81.

32. Neta C. Crawford and Audie Klotz, eds., *How Sanctions Work: Lessons from South Africa* (New York: St. Martin's Press, 1999). Richard N. Haas, ed., *Economic Sanctions and American Diplomacy* (New York: Council on Foreign Relations, distributed by Brookings Institution Press, 1998). Benjamin N. Judkins, "Economic Statecraft and Regime Type: Transparency, Credibility, and Conflict Resolution," paper presented at the annual meet-

ing of the International Studies Association, Portland, OR, 25 February—1 March 2003. Available electronically via http://www.isanet.org/portlandarchive/judkins.html.

33. David Cortright and George Lopez, "Assessing Smart Sanctions: Lessons from the 1990s," in *Smart Sanctions: Targeting Economic Statecraft*, ed. Cortright and Lopez (Lanham, MD: Rowman and Littlefield, 2002), 11–13.

34. The goal of the labor side accord is to "resolve issues in a cooperative manner." Under the agreement, a formal complaint leads to ministerial consultations and, if necessary, review by an "evaluation committee of experts." The committee issues reports/recommendations. Ultimately, an arbitral panel may be constituted to in turn set monetary sanctions and/or to order the suspension of trade privileges (the latter only in cases of disputes over occupational safety and health, child labor, or minimum wage). Corresponding text of the NAALC is available electronically via http://www.dol.gov/ILAB/media/reports/nao/naalcgd.htm#SubmissionsProcess.

35. Clifford Bob, *The Marketing of Rebellion: Insurgents, Media, and International Activism* (Cambridge: Cambridge University Press, 2005). Bob, "Merchants of Morality," *Foreign Policy* 129 (March/April 2002): 36–45. Bob, "Marketing Rebellion: Insurgent Groups, International Media, and NGO Support," *International Politics* 38 (September 2001): 311–34.

36. McAdam, Tarrow, and Tilly, *Dynamics of Contention*, 41.

37. Ibid., 44.

3. Child Labor, Child Rights, and Transnational Advocacy

1. The normative referents for children's rights vary. Among those specified in connection with this case are UN Declaration on the Rights of the Child (of 1959); ILO Convention 138 on Minimum Age (1973); UN Convention on the Rights of the Child (1989); and ILO Convention 182 on the Worst Forms of Child Labour (1999). Texts of ILO conventions can be accessed electronically via http://www.ilo.org.

2. *Congressional Record*, 100th Congress, 1st session, 14 July 1987, vol. 133, part 27:19818.

3. Memo from Bill Goold (assistant to Rep. Donald Pease, Democrat, Ohio) to Ed Long (assistant to Sen. Tom Harkin, Democrat, Iowa), 29 October 1987, photocopy. Unless otherwise noted, copies of original correspondence are on file with the author.

4. In May 1988, Bill Goold recommended changes in the Miller bill (HR 3112); see memo from Bill Goold to Rep. Donald Pease, 25 May 1988, photocopy. By July 1988, Reps. Pease and Miller requested that the House Subcommittee on Trade hold hearings on HR 3112. In June 1989, Reps. Pease, Tom Lantos, Charles Schumer, and Tony Hall urged colleagues in the House to support HR 3112. See letter from Representatives Pease, Lantos, Schumer, and Hall to members of the House of Representatives, 6 June 1989, photocopy. In November 1991, Rep. Pease and Rep. Tony Hall cosponsored the Child Labor Deterrence Act of 1991 (HR 3786), including provisions for country-wide import bans. For Pease's testimony before the House, see *Congressional Record*, 102nd Congress,1st session, 15 November 1991, vol. 137, part 25:32144.

5. Rosaline Costa, interview by the author, by telephone, 15 February 2002.

6. Ibid.

7. AFL-CIO, "Bangladesh," excerpt from 1990 GSP petition, photocopy on file with the author. AFL-CIO, "Bangladesh," brief statement opposing the 25 April 1991 decision by the United States Trade Representative to support GSP eligibility for Bangladesh, photocopy. Letter from Barbara Shailor/AFL-CIO to H. Jon Rosenbaum/USTR, 16 June 1999, and accompanying AFL-CIO petition, "Worker Rights and the Generalized System of Preferences: Bangladesh," AFL-CIO Petition to the Office of the United States Trade Representative, 16 June 1999. AFL-CIO, "Comments on Limitations of Duty-Free Treatment

on Imports from Bangladesh under the Generalized System of Preferences (as authorized under Title V of the Trade Act of 1974, as amended)," 15 August 2000, photocopy on file with the author. Ann Knipper (AFL-CIO), interview by the author, Washington, DC, 11 July 2001, and by telephone from New York City, 30 July 2002.

8. Women's Network–United Food and Commercial Workers Union, undated flyer on file with the author. Sonia Rosen, interview by the author, Washington, DC, 12 July 2001. Jo Boyden, Birgitta Ling, and William Myers, *What Works for Working Children* (Stockholm: Radda Barnen, 1998), 294.

9. For full text of the bill, introduced in the 102nd Congress of the United States, see http://thomas.loc.gov.

10. United States Congress, "Press Packet on Child Labor Reform Legislation," 18 March 1993, photocopy on file with the author. Senator Harkin's remarks are taken from his prepared speech, included in this press packet.

11. Ibid.

12. Shabbir Ahmed, interview by the author, Washington, DC, 18 March 2002.

13. International Labour Organization/International Programme on the Elimination of Child Labour (ILO/IPEC), "BGMEA, ILO, UNICEF Child Labor Project Bangladesh: Case Study or 'Midterm' Review," internal working paper prepared by Rijk van Haarlem, July 1997, 2, photocopy on file with the author.

14. "BGMEA Warns Members of Dire Consequences of Employing Children," *Morning Sun*, 31 December 1992.

15. ILO/IPEC, van Haarlem paper, 2. U.S. Department of Labor, *Advancing the Campaign against Child Labor: Efforts at the Country Level* (Washington, DC: U.S. Department of Labor, 2002), 28. Wahidur Rahman, "Paper for Roundtable Conference on Child Labor," hosted by ILO/IPEC, Dhaka, Bangladesh, undated photocopy on file with the author.

16. Export Promotion Bureau of Bangladesh 1997, cited in Najmir Nur Begum, "Women in Ready-Made Garment Industries: Issues and Concerns," unpublished working paper commissioned by the Ministry of Textiles, Textile Strategic Management Unit (Dhaka: Government of Bangladesh, 1997), 1, photocopy on file with the author.

17. Stanley A. Kochanek, "The Growing Commercialization of Power," in *Bangladesh: Promise and Performance,* ed. Rounaq Jahan (London: Zed Books, 2001), 154.

18. ILO/IPEC, van Haarlem paper, 2. See also Abu A. Abdullah, "Social Change and 'Modernization,' " in Jahan, *Bangladesh: Promise and Performance,* 129–47.

19. Begum, "Women in Ready-Made Garment Industries," 1.

20. ILO/IPEC, van Haarlem paper; Kochanek, " Growing Commercialization of Power."

21. Paula L. Green, "Child Labor Coalition May Seek Bangladesh Boycott," *Journal of Commerce,* 15 May 1995.

22. Debapriya Bhattacharya, "International Trade, Social Labelling and Developing Countries: The Case of Bangladesh's Garments Export and Use of Child Labor," in *Annuaire Suisse-Tiers Monde,* ed. J. Forster (Geneva: University Institute of Developing Studies, 1996), 215–38.

23. Farhad Mazhar, "Mr. Harkin's Talk of 'Human Rights'—or Scripture from the Mouth of Satan," *Ajker Kagoj,* 1993, undated text of a newspaper article translated and sent in email form by U.S. Embassy/Dhaka to William Melvin of the U.S. Information Agency, 12 August 1993.

24. "New Challenge for Garments Industry," *Daily Star,* 2 January 1993.

25. Shakeel Anwar, partial photocopy of an undated news article on file with the author.

26. Lippi, forty-year-old domestic servant and household head, quoted in Emily Delap, "Economic and Cultural Forces in the Child Labour Debate: Evidence from Urban Bangladesh," *Journal of Development Studies* 37, no. 4 (April 2001): 1–22.

27. "On the Question of Child Labor," *Janakantha*, 5 August 1993, text of a newspaper article translated and sent in email form by U.S. Embassy/Dhaka to William Melvin, 12 August 1993.

28. "Child Labor and International Law," *Dainik Bangla*, 8 August 1993, text of a newspaper article translated and sent in email form by U.S. Embassy/Dhaka to William Melvin, 12 August 1993.

29. This and successive quotes from Nur Khan Liton are from her article "Harkin's Law: More Harm Than Good," *Dhaka Courier*, 18 September 1993, reprinted in Ain-O-Salish Kendra (ASK), *Rights and Realities* (Dhaka: ASK, September 1997).

30. This and succeeding quotes regarding Collingsworth are from a cable from U.S. Embassy/Dhaka to U.S. Information Agency, 5 August 1993, "Subject: Voluntary Speaker Terry Collingsworth," Reference USIA 31655.

31. "Activists Blast US Bill on Child Labor," United Press International, 8 August 1993.

32. Co-hosts of the press conference included the organization Sram Bikash Kendra (represented by Ms. Farida Akter); Ain-O-Salish Kendra (represented by Hameeda Hossain); Karmojibi Nari (represented by Shirin Akhter), and National Garments Sramik Federation. For further detail, see cable from U.S. Embassy/Dhaka to U.S. Information Agency, 9 August 1993, "Subject: Bangladesh Media Reaction."

33. Hameeda Hossain, interview by the author, by email, 3 February 2002.

34. Suraiya Haque, interview by the author, by email, 27 May 2002.

35. Zina D'Costa, interview by the author, by email, 28 May 2002.

36. ILO/IPEC, van Haarlem paper, 3.

37. Margaret Keck and Kathryn Sikkink, "Transnational Advocacy Networks in International and Regional Politics," *International Social Science Journal* 159 (1999): 89–101, especially p. 98.

38. Tim Noonan, interview by the author, by telephone from New York City, 1 March 2002.

39. Terry Collingsworth, interview by the author, Washington, DC, 15 August 2001.

40. Sonia Rosen, interviews by the author, in Washington, DC, 12 July 2001 and 19 March 2002.

41. Andrew Samet, interview by the author, Washington, DC, 10 May 2002.

42. Ruby Nobel, interview by the author, by email, 27 May 2002.

43. Birgitta Ling, interview by the author, by email, 13 December 2001.

44. ILO/IPEC, van Haarlem paper, 3.

45. Rosaline Costa, email to the author, 13 August 2002. See also Michael E. Nielsen, "The Politics of Corporate Responsibility and Child Labour in the Bangladeshi Garment Industry," *International Affairs* 81, no. 3 (2005): 559–80, especially p. 576.

46. U.S. Department of Labor, Bureau of International Labor Affairs, *By the Sweat and Toil of Children*, vol. 1: *The Use of Child Labor in U.S. Manufactured and Mined Imports* (Washington, DC: Department of Labor, International Labor Affairs Bureau, 1994). The series includes seven reports, the last published in 2002.

47. U.S. Congress, House of Representatives, Office of Rep. Tom Harkin, "Harkin Study Confirms Use of Child Labor in US Imports," press release, 19 September 1994, photocopy on file with the author.

48. Sumaira Chowdhury, "When Motives Matter: The 1993 Child Labor Deterrence Act and the Memorandum of Understanding" (undergraduate thesis, Wellesley College, 1998), 34. See also Timothy A. Glut, "Changing the Approach to Ending Child Labor: An International Solution to an International Problem," *Vanderbilt Journal of Transnational Law* 28 (1996): 1203–44.

49. Pharis Harvey's longstanding role in labor rights activism is discussed in Robin Broad, ed., *Global Backlash: Citizen Initiatives for a Just World Economy* (Lanham, MD: Rowman and Littlefield, 2002), 119.

50. Pharis Harvey, "Press Statement: Labor Rights Fund Urges Passage of Re-introduced International Child Labor Deterrence Act," International Labor Rights Fund, 18 March 1993, photocopy on file with the author. For a timeline and analysis of negotiations, see Nielsen, " Politics of Corporate Responsibility," 569–71.

51. Reported in Pharis Harvey, "Historic Breakthrough for Bangladesh Kids Endangered by Industry Inaction," *Worker Rights News*, no. 12 (August 1995): 1, 5, 6.

52. See letters from Pharis Harvey to Redwan Ahmed, 14 and 19 April 1995.

53. See fax from Pharis Harvey and Linda Golodner (co-chairs, Child Labor Coalition) to Child Labor Coalition membership, 18 May 1995.

54. See letter from Pharis Harvey to Redwan Ahmed (chair, BGMEA), 20 May 1995.

55. See letter from Pharis Harvey to Redwan Ahmed, 26 May 1995, on file with the author.

56. Darlene Adkins, interview by the author, by telephone, 13 March 2001.

57. See letter from Pharis Harvey and Linda Golodner to Gail Dorn (vice president, Dayton Hudson Corporation), dated 2 June 1995.

58. See memo from Darlene Adkins to "friends" of the Child Labor Coalition, 29 June 1995.

59. Ethel Brooks, "The Consumer's New Clothes: Global Protest, the New International Division of Labor, and Women's Work in the Garment Industry" (Ph.D. diss., New York University, 2000), 90–124.

60. Memo from Andrew Samet to Peter Reinecke, 26 June 1995.

61. ILO, International Programme for the Elimination of Child Labor (IPEC), *The Memorandum of Understanding (MOU) between BGMEA, ILO, and UNICEF: A "Quick Reference" Pamphlet* (Dhaka, Bangladesh: ILO/IPEC, October 1996). A year after the MOU was signed, the U.S. government made an $876,000 contribution to IPEC for Bangladesh programs. See U.S. Department of Labor, "Labor Department Funds Governments for the Eradication of Child Labor," news release 96–207, 30 May 1996, photocopy on file with the author.

62. National Consumers League, "Consumer Boycott Spurs Responsible End to Child Labor," *NCL Bulletin* 57, no. 3 (May-June-July 1995): 1, 9.

63. Wage estimates are based on data gathered from 1996 to 1999 by research teams funded as part of a United Kingdom Department for International Development study, cited in Emily Delap, "Economic and Cultural Forces in the Child Labour Debate." See also Mohammad M. Rahman, Rasheda Khanan, and Nur Uddin Absar, "Child Labor in Bangladesh: A Critical Appraisal of Harkin's Bill and the MOU-Type Schooling Program," *Journal of Economic Issues* 1, no. 33 (December 1999): 874–1003.

64. See two separate letters from Pharis Harvey and Linda Golodner to Redwan Ahmed, each dated 4 July 1995. See also Child Labor Coalition, press release, 6 July 1995, photocopy on file with the author.

65. Figures vary for the actual number of factories surveyed and number of children identified. Rijk van Haarlem of the ILO cites a figure of 2,152 factories surveyed and 10,546 children identified. See ILO/IPEC, van Haarlem report, 5. Estimates from UNICEF are of 1,821 factories surveyed and 12,000 children identified. See UNICEF, unpublished "Report on Status of Implementation of the MOU: Monthly Report—As of 26 November 1995," faxed with a cover letter from Gretchen Goodale (UNICEF/Bangladesh) to Pharis Harvey, 3 December 1995.

66. U.S. Department of Labor, *Advancing the Campaign against Child Labor*, 30.

67. The actual number of children working in the garment sector was considerably higher than the small sample ultimately identified in the 1995 survey. Harvey, "Historic Breakthrough for Bangladesh Kids," 1.

68. Darlene Adkins, interview by the author, by telephone, 13 March 2001.

69. Abdul Hai, interview by the author, by telephone from New York City, 29 April 2002.

70. Bangladesh is the seventh most densely populated country in the world. The Economist, *Pocket World in Figures: 2002 Edition* (London: Profile Books, 2002), 16.

71. Shabbir Ahmed, interview by the author, Washington, DC, 18 March 2002.

72. Mustafa Kamal, interview by the author, Washington, DC, 19 March 2002.

73. Nazrul Islam Khan, interview by the author, by email, 11 December 2001. European trade unions echo this emphasis. Neil Kearney (director general, International Textile, Garment and Leather Workers' Federation/ITGLWF), interview by the author, New York City, 1 March 2002. Tim Noonan (International Confederation of Free Trade Unions/ICFTU), interview by the author, by telephone from New York City, 1 March 2002. Steve Grinter (education secretary, ITGLWF), interview by the author, by telephone from New York City, 8 February 2002.

74. Nilima Chawla, *In Search of the Best Interests of the Child: A First Step towards Eliminating Child Labour in the Bangladesh Garment Industry* (Dhaka: UNICEF, October 1996), 5, 11, 31.

75. International Labour Organization, "A Future without Child Labour: Global Report under the Follow-up to the ILO Declaration on Fundamental Principles and Rights at Work," prepared for the International Labour Conference, 90th session, 2002, report I-B, Geneva, 1.

76. George Tsebelis developed the concept of "nested" explanations for political outcomes (albeit under more highly restrictive conditions) in *Nested Games: Rational Choice in Comparative Politics* (Berkeley: University of California Press, 1990).

77. Chowdhury, "When Motives Matter."

78. Bangladesh ranks 139th out of 177 countries assessed by the UN Development Programme (UNDP) in its annual *Human Development Report 2005* (New York: Oxford University Press, 2005), 221. See also Binayak Sen, "Growth, Poverty and Human Development," in Jahan, *Bangladesh: Promise and Performance*, 267–308.

79. Kim Moody, *Workers in a Lean World: Unions in the International Economy* (New York: Verso Books, 1997). Ronaldo Munck and Peter Waterman, eds., *Labor Worldwide in an Era of Globalization* (New York: St. Martin's Press, 1999). Andrew Ross, ed., *No Sweat: Fashion, Free Trade and the Rights of Garment Workers* (London: Verso, 1997).

80. UNICEF, *Poverty and Children: Lessons of the 90s for Least Developed Countries* (New York: UNICEF, May 2001), 20.

81. Maria Patricia Fernandez-Kelly, *For We Are Sold, I and My People: Women and Industry in Mexico's Frontier* (Albany: State University of New York Press, 1983). Brooks, "Consumer's New Clothes." Radhika Balikrishnan, *The Hidden Assembly Line: Gender Dynamics of Subcontracted Work in a Global Economy* (Bloomfield, CT: Kumarian Press, 2002).

82. Charlotte Bunch, *Demanding Accountability: The Global Campaign and Vienna Tribunal for Women's Human Rights* (New Brunswick, NJ: Center for Women's Global Leadership, Douglass College, Rutgers University; New York: United Nations Development Fund for Women, 1994).

83. Caroline Thomas, "International Financial Institutions and Social and Economic Human Rights: An Exploration," in *Human Rights Fifty Years On: A Reappraisal*, ed. Tony Evans (Manchester: Manchester University Press, 1998), 161–85. Association for Women's Rights in Development (AWID), "The International Covenant on Economic, Social and Cultural Rights," *Women's Rights and Economic Change—Facts and Issues* 3 (August 2002): 1–8.

84. "The Other Government in Bangladesh," *The Economist*, 25 July 1998, 42. See also Sajeda Amin and Cynthia B. Lloyd, "Women's Lives and Rapid Fertility Decline: Some Lessons from Bangladesh and Egypt," Population Council Working Papers series, no. 117 (New York: Population Council, 1998), 34–40.

4. Discrimination, the Right to Work, and Reproductive Freedom

1. Article 170(II) of the Ley Federal del Trabajo (LFT) guarantees women six weeks of paid maternity leave before delivery and six weeks afterward. Unless she has consistently paid into the social security system, a pregnant worker's employer must assume responsibility for her salary during this period. Full text of related laws is available electronically via http://www.cddhcu.gob.mx/leyinfo/pdf/125.pdf.

2. The term *maquiladora* is derived from the Spanish colonial term *maquila*, the portion of wheat, grain, or oil given to a miller each time he/she finished milling a product. Román García-Pelayo y Gross, *Pequeño Larousse ilustrado* (Barcelona: Ediciones Larousse, 1989), 658.

3. Aureliano González-Baz, "Manufacturing in Mexico: The Mexican In-Bond (*Maquila*) Program," available electronically via http://www.udel.edu/leipzig/texts2/vox128.htm.

4. United States Central Intelligence Agency, *CIA Factbook 2001*, available electronically via http://www.cia.gov/cia/publications/factbook/. Catalina Denman, "*Maquiladoras* and Health on the US-Mexico Border: Challenges for Research and Action," talk delivered at the Institute of Latin American Studies, Columbia University, New York City, 14 October 2002. Héctor Vázquez-Tercero, "Medición de flujo de divisas de la balanza comercial de México" [Measurement of the flow of earnings of Mexico's commercial balance], *Comercio Exterior* 40, no. 10 (October 2000): 890–94.

5. For detailed wage data, see Ruth Rosenbaum, *Making the Invisible Visible: A Study of Purchasing Power of Maquila Workers in Mexico 2000* (Hartford, CT: Center for Reflection, Education and Action, 2000), 15, 69–70.

6. Human Rights Watch, acknowledgments, *No Guarantees: Sex Discrimination in Mexico's Maquiladora Sector* (New York: HRW 1996), 57. Hereafter referred to as HRW *No Guarantees* 1996.

7. LaShawn Jefferson, interview by the author, Washington, DC, 14 March 2000.

8. Widney Brown, interview by the author, New York City, 24 August 2001.

9. Pharis Harvey, interview by the author, Washington, DC, 14 March 2000.

10. HRW *No Guarantees* 1996, 36–44. A similar sample of people was interviewed for this book, including representatives of the JCA at both the state and federal levels, and representatives of the STPS at the state and federal levels. Gerardo Medel-Torres (JCA–Baja California), interview by the author, Tijuana, Baja California, 4 October 2001; Jesús Terán-Martínez (JCA-Tamaulipas), interview by the author, Matamoros, Tamaulipas, 11 January 2002; Guillermo Hernández-Gallindo (federal JCA, Hermosillo offices), interview by the author, Hermosillo, Sonora, 23 October 2001; Victoria Vásquez-Rosas (STPS–Baja California), interview by the author, Mexicali, Baja California, 1 October 2001; Sandra Clementina Castro and Julio Villarreal-Aguirre (STPS-Sonora), interview by the author, Hermosillo, Sonora, 22 October 2001; and Ana Berta Colín (federal STPS, Mexico City headquarters), interview by the author, Mexico City, 18 January 2002.

11. HRW *No Guarantees* 1996, 45–54.

12. HRW *No Guarantees* 1996.

13. Ibid., 37.

14. Among others, Mexico has ratified the Convention on the Elimination of Discrimination against Women (CEDAW); the International Covenant on Civil and Political Rights; the International Covenant on Economic, Social and Cultural Rights; ILO Convention 111 on Discrimination; and the American Convention on Human Rights.

15. Julia Quiñónez, interview by the author, Piedras Negras, Coahuila, 8 January 2002. For background on the Comité Fronterizo de Obreras, see Rachel Kamel and Anya Hoffman, eds., *The Maquiladora Reader: Cross-Border Organizing since NAFTA* (Philadelphia: American Friends Service Committee, 1999), 89–96.

16. Carmen Valadéz-Prez, interview by the author, Tijuana, Baja California, 27 September 2001. See also Carmen Valadéz-Prez, "Mexico: NAFTA versus Human Rights," in *Women's Lives in the New Global Economy*, ed. Penny Duggan and Heather Dashner, Notebook for Study and Research no. 22 (Amsterdam: International Institute for Research and Education, 1994), 51–55.

17. María Santos-Ramírez, interview by the author, Tijuana, Baja California, 19 September 2001. Elsa Jiménez, interview by the author, Tijuana, Baja California, 26 September 2001.

18. Pheng Cheah, "Posit(ion)ing Human Rights in the Current Global Conjuncture," *Public Culture* 9 (1997): 233–66, and Inderpal Grewal, "'Women's Rights as Human Rights': Feminist Practices, Global Feminism, and Human Rights Regimes in Transnationality," *Citizenship Studies* 3, no. 3 (1999): 337–54.

19. Focus group with CFO members, conducted by the author in Piedras Negras, Coahila, 8 January 2002. Focus group with DODS members, conducted by the author in Reynosa, Tamaulipas, 10 January 2002.

20. Focus group conducted by the author in Agua Prieta, Sonora, 16 January 2002.

21. The pregnancy screening complaint submitted in 1997 is hereafter referred to as "Submission 9701," using the number assigned it by the US-NAO. Full text can be accessed electronically via http://www.dol.gov/ILAB/media/reports/nao/submissions/Sub9701.htm.

22. This research is described in a follow-up report: Human Rights Watch, *A Job or Your Rights: Continued Sex Discrimination in Mexico's Maquiladora Sector* (New York: HRW, 1998), 3. Hereafter referred to as HRW *A Job or Your Rights* 1998.

23. Participants in the hearing included LaShawn Jefferson and Joel Solomon (HRW); Ed Krueger (then of the American Friends Service Committee); Terry Collingsworth (ILRF); María Estela Ríos (former president, ANAD) and six workers from CFO. See United States National Administrative Office (US-NAO), "Witnesses, Public Hearing on Submission No. 9701, Brownsville, Texas, 19 November 1997," undated photocopy obtained through the US-NAO.

24. US-NAO, Bureau of International Labor Affairs, United States Department of Labor, *Public Report of Review of NAO Submission no. 9701*, dated 12 January 1998. Full text of this report can be accessed ·electronically via http://www.dol.gov/ILAB/media/reports/nao/pubrep9701.htm.

25. María Santos-Ramírez, interview by the author, Tijuana, Baja California, 19 September 2001.

26. Julia Quiñónez, interview by the author, Piedras Negras, Coahuila, 8 January 2002.

27. See Mujeres Trabajadoras Unidas, AC/Mujeres en Acción Sindical (MUTUAC/MAS), DIVERSAS, Centro de Investigación y Estudio de la Sexualidad (CIESEX), Equidad y Género, and Grupo de Información en Reproducción Elegida (GIRE), *Cartilla: Maternidad y Trabajo—Pueden conciliarse?* undated pamphlet, 19–20.

28. Government of Mexico, Secretaría del Trabajo y Previsión Social (Mexicali), "Reformas a la Ley del Seguro Social: Programa de Lactancia Corporativa y Hostigamiento Sexual," May 2001, 3, photocopy on file with the author. The STPS explored possible reforms of Mexican law on maternity benefits (i.e., Social Security Law, articles 101 and 107) and conducted national consultations to solicit opinions on how to apportion state, employer, and employee contributions to maternity benefits differently; this report was produced thereafter.

29. Amelia Iruretagoyena, interview by the author, Hermosillo, Sonora, 22 October 2001.

30. Pilar Muriedas, interview by the author, Mexico City, 18 January 2002.

31. Yolanda Ramírez and Melisa Villaescusa, interview by the author, Mexico City, 15

January 2002. The Dutch government funded MUTUAC/MAS, DIVERSAS, CIESEX, Equidad y Género, and GIRE to work on the 1998 campaign.

32. The aim of these grants was to influence international development and trade policies from a critical human rights perspective. Ana Luisa Liguori, interview by the author, Mexico City, 14 January 2002.

33. Yolanda Ramírez, interview by the author, Mexico City, 15 January 2002.

34. Patricia Mercado, interview by the author, Mexico City, 15 January 2002.

35. Yolanda Ramírez, interview by the author, Mexico City, 15 January 2002.

36. Linda Stevenson, "Confronting Gender Discrimination in the Mexican Workplace: Women Taking Action in Local, National, and Transnational Policy Arenas," in "Gender Politics and Policy Process in Mexico, 1968–2000: Symbolic Gains for Women in an Emerging Democracy" (Ph.D. diss., University of Pittsburgh, 2000), 7.

37. Eloísa Aguirre, interview by the author, Hermosillo, Sonora, 22 October 2001.

38. Elsa Jiménez-Larios, interview by the author, Tijuana, Baja California, 26 September 2001.

39. Diana Velasco, "Despidos por embarazo en la mujer, no se denuncia en 90% de los casos," El Día, 21 October 1998.

40. Fabiola Martínez, "Convocan a foro de conciliación entre la maternidad y el trabajo," La Jornada, 22 October 1998.

41. Some 567 people were informally surveyed; 51 percent of those responding were women, 49 percent men. Monica Martín, "Iniciativa para evitar que el embarazo sea causa de despido," publication name unavailable, 22 October 1998, photocopy on file with the author. Miguel Salazar, "Denuncian aplicación de exámen de no gravidez en mujeres recién contratadas," El Sol de México, 22 October 1998.

42. Fabiola Martinez, "Convocan a foro." See also MUTUAC/MAS, DIVERSAS, CIESEX, Equidad y Género, and GIRE, "Resúmen de casos presentados en el marco del Tribunal de Conciliación entre la Maternidad y el Trabajo," unpublished collection of testimony presented at the tribunal, Mexico City, 22 October 1998, photocopy on file with the author.

43. Ibid.

44. Ana Luisa Cárdenas of the Partido Revolucionario Democrático (PRD) and Angélica Luna Parra of the Partido Revolucionario Institucional (PRI) called, respectively, for legislative changes and for private sector incentives to end pregnancy screening. See Liliana Alcántara, "Se unen legisladoras al apoyo a trabajadoras embarazadas," El Universal, 22 October 1998.

45. The bilateral consultations are referenced in a report by the US-NAO, "Status of Submissions under the North American Agreement on Labor Cooperation," updated 11 January 2000, 4; available from the US-NAO in photocopy form. Text of the implementing agreement reached by the U.S. and Mexican governments is available in the appendix to HRW A Job or Your Rights 1998, 79. Notably, the implementing agreement commits Mexico to address only "post-hire" pregnancy discrimination.

46. HRW A Job or Your Rights 1998.

47. Letter from Regan Ralph (Human Rights Watch), Pharis Harvey (International Labor Rights Fund), Óscar Alzaga-Sánchez (Asociación Nacional de Abogados Democráticos), and José Miguel Vivanco (HRW) to Alexis Herman (U.S. secretary of labor), 23 February 1999 Unless otherwise noted, copies of original correspondence are on file with the author.

48. "Las maquiladoras, espejismo ante el desempleo," Diario Yucatán, 3 March 1999. See Teresa Ochoa, "Denuncian discriminación," Reforma, 3 March 1999.

49. US-NAO, "Status of Submissions under the North American Agreement on Labor Cooperation, " updated 11 January 2000, 4 (available from the US-NAO in photocopy form).

50. Claudia Herrera-Beltrán, "Eliminan el certificado de ingravidez para mujeres en educación," *La Jornada*, 21 May 1999. See also "Género: Avances de la igualdad," *La Jornada*, 22 May 1999.

51. Human Rights Watch, *World Report 2000* (New York: HRW, 2000).

52. For a summary of forty-nine bills presented from 1997 to 2000, six of which focused directly on pregnancy-related discrimination, see Consorcio para el Diálogo Parlamentario y la Equidad, "La equidad de género en la LVII legislatura," *Agenda Afirmativa*, undated pamphlet on file with the author.

53. Human Rights Watch, *Trading Away Rights: The Unfulfilled Promise of NAFTA's Labor Side Agreement*, vol. 13, no. 2 B (April 2001).

54. Elsa Jiménez-Larios, interview by the author, Tijuana, Baja California, 26 September 2001.

55. Julia Quiñónez, interview by the author, Piedras Negras, Coahuila, 8 January 2002.

56. Antanacio Martínez, interview by the author, Río Bravo, Tamaulipas, 10 January 2002.

57. Marcia Contreras-López, interview by the author, Hermosillo, Sonora, 1 November 2001.

58. Teresa Hernández, interview by the author, Matamoros, Tamaulipas, 11 January 2002.

59. Minerva Nájara-Nájara, interview by the author, Tijuana, Baja California, 3 October 2001; Elsa Jiménez-Larios, interview by the author, Tijuana, Baja California, 26 September 2001; Mireya Scarone-Adarga, interview by the author, Hermosillo, Sonora, 17 October 2001; Jacobo Fonseca, interview by the author, Piedras Negras, Coahuila, 8 January 2002.

60. HRW *A Job or Your Rights* 1998, 4.

61. Mireya Scarone-Adarga, "Prohibido embarazarse: los derechos reproductivos de las trabajadoras en Hermosillo" (B.A. thesis, Universidad de Sonora, 2001), 60. Scarone-Adarga, a member of Mujeres en Acción Sindical and former director of the Casa de la Mujer of Hermosillo, led regional efforts in the 1998 campaign in the state of Sonora.

62. For Mexican activists involved in both campaigns, reproductive rights are defined varyingly. A woman's "autonomous decision to determine her productive processes" is one common definition. See CIESEX, MUTUAC-MAS, GIRE, "Propuestas de reforma a la Ley Federal del Trabajo para desalentar la práctica del despido por embarazo y los exámenes de no gravidez," unpublished document, 1, photocopy on file with the author.

63. Leticia R. Cuevas with Kathlene McDonald, "Analysis of Issues Raised in Submission 9701, Gender Discrimination and Pregnancy Based Discrimination," unpublished manuscript dated December 1997, available electronically via http://www.dol.gov/ILAB/media/reports/nao/9701analysis.htm

64. Cuevas, "Analysis of Issues Raised in Submission 9701," 11, cites legal commentary on the 1917 decision by Mexico's constitutional drafters to remove labor from the country's Federal Civil Code and to incorporate it within the Constitution under a separate chapter (now article 123) on the right to work.

65. Cuevas (in "Analysis of Issues Raised in Submission 9701," 5, 18) cites article 4 of the Mexican Constitution and article 154 of Mexico's Federal Labor Law as giving preference to sole wage earners. She provides detail on the increase over time in the number of Mexican women who are primary wage earners, particularly in the maquiladora industry, citing Cirila Quintero-Ramírez, "Participación femenina en las maquiladoras: reconsideraciones y nuevas hipóteses," paper presented at First Congress on Women's Studies in the North of Mexico and South of the United States, El Colegio de la Frontera Norte, Matamoros campus, Monterrey, Nuevo León, 23–25 October 1997, 3 (cited in Cuevas, "Analysis of Issues Raised in Submission 9701," 24).

66. MUTUAC/MAS et al., *Cartilla*. See also Rubén García, "Crear tribunal contra la marginación a mujeres, piden ONGs," *El Nacional*, 6 March 1998.

67. Erika Cervantes, "Nueva identidad: los derechos de las mujeres al interior de las familias," publication title unavailable, February 1998. Reprinted in Casa de la Mujer–Hermosillo, "8 de Marzo, Día internacional de la mujer," undated photocopy on file with the author.

68. CIESEX, MUTUAC-MAS, GIRE, "Propuestas de reforma a la Ley Federal del Trabajo para desalentar la práctica del despido por embarazo y los exámenes de no gravidez," 1.

69. Elena Tapia, "Reproducción humana: una responsabilidad social," opening remarks delivered at the Tribunal on Reconciling Maternity and Work, Mexico City, 22 October 1998.

70. María Luisa Sánchez-Fuentes, closing remarks delivered at the Tribunal on Reconciling Maternity and Work, Mexico City, 22 October 1998.

71. Casa de la Mujer–Hermosillo, "Mujeres trabajadoras en Sonora: Algunas consideraciones a tomarse en cuenta para elaborar un pliego petitorio de trabajadoras en el estado," undated photocopy on file with the author.

72. CIESEX and DIVERSA, "Comunicado de Prensa," CIESEX-DIVERSA/COM002, Mexico City, 5 March 1998, photocopy on file with the author.

73. Claudia Rodríguez-Santiago, "Discriminan a las damas en algunos centros de trabajo," publication title unavailable, 6 March 1998, photocopy on file with the author.

74. Columbia University, Center for the Study of Human Rights, *Woman and Human Rights: The Basic Documents* (New York: Columbia University, 1996), 62–63.

75. Delegates to the UN International Conference on Population and Development at Cairo (1994) called for the elimination of "discriminatory practices by employers against women, such as requiring tests for contraceptive use or statements about pregnancy," cited in Scarone-Adarga, "Prohibido embarazarse: los derechos reproductivos de las trabajadoras en Hermosillo," 99.

76. See ILO Convention 158, article 5(b), available electronically via http://www.ilo .org/ilolex/english/convdisp1.htm. Demand for ratification of this ILO convention is included in a press release produced by the campaign in conjunction with International Women's Day, March 1998. See CIESEX and DIVERSA, "Comunicado de Prensa," 5 March 1998. See also Berta Fernández, "Piden eliminar la discriminación que sufren las mujeres embarazadas en sus empleos," *El Universal*, 6 March 1998. Jesús Cervantes, "Crearán un tribunal para denunciar despidos por embarazo," *La Jornada*, 6 March 1998.

77. Cuevas, "Analysis of Issues Raised in Submission 9701," 96.

78. Scarone-Adarga, "Prohibido embarazarse: los derechos reproductivos de las trabajadoras en Hermosillo," 90–98.

79. CIESEX, DIVERSA, MUTUAC-MAS, GIRE, and Unión de Trabajadoras Mexicanas (UTM), "Campaña para desalentar la práctica del despido por maternidad y el exámen de no embarazo," undated fact sheet, photocopy on file with the author.

80. Velasco, "Despidos por embarazo en la mujer, no se denuncia."

81. Cited in Cuevas, "Analysis of Issues Raised in Submission 9701," 92, 94.

82. Gerardo Medel-Torres, interview by the author, Tijuana, Baja California, 4 October 2001.

83. Letter from Julio C. Villarreal-Aguirre to Mireya Scarone-Adarga, dated 9 July 2001, cited in Scarone-Adarga, "Prohibido embarazarse: los derechos reproductivos de las trabajadoras en Hermosillo," 86.

84. Patricia Mercado, interview by the author, Mexico City, 15 January 2002. Melisa Villaescusa and Yolanda Ramírez, interview by the author, Mexico City, 15 January 2002. Pilar Muriedas, interview by the author, Mexico City, 18 January 2002.

85. Milisa Villaescusa and Yolanda Ramírez, interview by the author, Mexico City, 15 January 2002.

86. Cuevas develops this argument based on analysis of International Labour Organization (ILO), *Fighting Discrimination in Employment and Occupation* (Geneva: Imprimerie Corbaz, SA, 1968), 41, cited in Cuevas, "Analysis of Issues Raised in Submission 9701," 51; and Leticia Bonifaz-Alonso, *El problema de la eficacia en el derecho* (Mexico City: Editorial Porrúa, 1993), 185, cited in Cuevas, "Analysis of Issues Raised in Submission 9701," 53.

87. Marcia Contreras-López, interview by the author, Hermosillo, Sonora, 1 November 2001.

88. Jaime Villalpando, interview by the author, Tijuana, Baja California, 3 October 2001.

89. These observations are based on findings from fifteen interviews and two focus groups conducted by the author with members of NGOs from the states of Baja California and Sonora during the period September to November 2001; from eight interviews and two focus groups conducted with members of NGOs from Coahuila and Tamaulipas during January 2002; and from seven interviews conducted with NGOs from Mexico City in January 2002.

90. Letter from LaShawn Jefferson (HRW) to Carmen Valadéz (Factor X), dated 8 May 1997.

91. Blanca Torres, interview by the author, Mexico City, 14 January 2002. For a more general discussion, see Jonathan Fox, "State-Society Relations in Mexico: Historical Legacies and Contemporary Trends," *Latin American Research Review* 35, no. 2 (2000): 183–203.

92. Frans Ingelberts, interview by the author, Piedras Negras, Coahuila, 8 January 2002.

93. Arturo Solís, interview by the author, Reynosa, Tamaulipas, 10 January 2002.

94. Julia Quiñónez, interview by the author, Piedras Negras, Coahuila, 8 January 2002.

95. Carmen Valadéz, interview by the author, Tijuana, Baja California, 27 September 2001.

96. Patricia Mercado, interview by the author, Mexico City, 15 January 2002.

97. Cuevas, "Analysis of Issues Raised in Submission 9701," 11.

98. Nora Hamilton, *The Limits of State Autonomy: Post-Revolutionary Mexico* (Princeton: Princeton University Press, 1982), 60–61.

99. Full text of the Federal Labor Law (Ley Federal del Trabajo, or LFT) is available electronically via http://www.cddhcu.gob.mx/leyinfo/.

100. Coalition for Justice in the Maquiladoras, *Guía para la Ley Federal del Trabajo, parte 1 y parte 2* (San Antonio, TX: Coalition for Justice in the Maquiladoras, 1997), part 1, pp. 30–31.

101. Full text of article 102(B) is available electronically via http://www.cddhcu.gob .mx/leyinfo/pdf/1.pdf. Full text of the Ley de la Comisión Nacional de Derechos Humanos is available electronically via http://www.cddhcu.gob.mx/leyinfo/pdf/47 .pdf.

102. Ana Berta Atuñes, interview by the author, Hermosillo, Sonora, 31 October 2001.

103. Procuraduría de los Derechos Humanos y Protección Ciudadana del Estado de Baja California, "Mensaje del Procurador de Los Derechos Humanos, C. Raúl Ramírez Baena: La larga lucha por los Derechos Sociales," *Gaceta*, January–September 2001, 4–5.

104. Articles 164–72 of the Federal Labor Law of Mexico are available electronically via http://www.cddhcu.gob.mx/leyinfo/pdf/125.pdf.

105. Letter from LaShawn Jefferson (HRW) to Carmen Valadéz (Factor X), dated 24 July 1995.

106. Lewis Karesh, interview by the author, Washington, DC, 15 March 2000.

107. United States Department of State, Bureau of Democracy, Human Rights and

Labor, "Mexico Country Report on Human Rights Practices for 1998," released 26 February 1999, and "Mexico Country Report on Human Rights Practices for 1999," released 25 February 2000.

108. United Nations, *Report of the Committee on the Elimination of Discrimination against Women* (eighteenth and nineteenth sessions), General Assembly, Official Records, 53rd session, supplement no. 38 (A/53/38/Rev.1). United Nations, "Entrenched attitudes must be uprooted for Mexican women to advance, women's anti-discrimination committee told," press release (WOM/1019), 30 January 1998. United Nations, "Progress made in advancement of Mexican women, but changes not yet 'radical,' anti-discrimination committee told," press release (WOM/1020), 30 January 1998. United Nations, Committee on the Rights of the Child, *Summary record of the 569th meeting, Committee on the Rights of the Child, [Second periodic report of] Mexico*, twenty-second session, 27 September 1999 (CRC/C/SR.569), distributed 5 October 1999, available electronically via http://www.unhchr.ch/tbs/doc.nsf/.

109. Mireya Scarone, interview by the author, Hermosillo, Sonora, 17 October 2001. Yolanda Ramírez-León and Melisa Villaescusa, interview by the author, Mexico City, 15 January 2002.

110. Ana Luisa Liguori, interview by the author, Mexico City, 14 January 2002. Blanca Lomeli and Liliana Andrade, interview by the author, Tijuana, Baja California, 25 September 2001.

111. Sidney Tarrow defines a repertoire of contention as "at once a structural and a cultural concept, involving not only what people *do* when they are engaged in conflict with others, but what they *know how to do* and what others *expect* them to do" (emphasis in original). Sidney Tarrow, *Power in Movement: Social Movements and Contentious Politics*, 2nd ed. (Cambridge, UK: Cambridge University Press, 1998), 30. See also Charles Tilly, *From Mobilization to Revolution* (Reading, MA: Addison-Wesley, 1978); Tilly, *Popular Contention in Great Britain 1758–1834* (Cambridge: Harvard University Press, 1995); Marc Traugott, *Repertoires and Cycles of Collective Action* (Durham, NC: Duke University Press, 1995).

5. A Decade Later

1. These categories draw on Jonathan Fox, "Lessons from Mexico-US Civil Society Coalitions," in *Cross Border Dialogues: US-Mexico Social Movement Networking*, ed. David Brooks and Jonathan Fox (La Jolla, CA: Center for US-Mexican Studies, University of California–San Diego, 2002), 386–87.

2. Ibid., 387.

3. See the "Socially Responsive Programs" section of the website of the Bangladesh Garment Manufacturers and Exporters Association: http://www.bgmea.com/social.htm.

4. Centre for Policy Dialogue, *Phasing Out of the Apparel Quota: Addressing Livelihood Concerns in Bangladesh* (Dhaka, Bangladesh: University Press Limited, 2003), 30.

5. South Asian Association for Regional Cooperation (SAARC), "Third SAARC Ministerial Conference on Children, 20–22 August 1996, Rawalpindi: Background Notes" (Rawalpindi, Pakistan: UNICEF ROSA, October 1997), 59. Hereafter referred to as SAARC Third Ministerial Background Notes.

6. References to the Rawalpindi Resolution appear in the opening introductory paragraph of the report (p. 1) and in a section titled "Children in Situations of Exploitation, including Physical and Psychological Recovery and Reintegration" (71). For full report, see United Nations, Committee on the Rights of the Child, "Consideration of Reports Submitted by States Parties under Article 44 of the Convention [on the Rights of

the Child]," CRC/C/65/Add.22, 14 March 2003. Hereafter referred to as UNCRC Bangladesh Second Report. Available electronically via http://www.hri.ca/forthe record2003/documentation/tbodies/crc-c-65–add22.htm.

7. Mohammad M. Rahman, Rasheda Khanan, and Nur Uddin Absar, "Child Labor in Bangladesh: A Critical Appraisal of Harkin's Bill and the MOU-Type Schooling Program," *Journal of Economic Issues* 1, no. 33 (December 1999): 874–1003. Munir Quddus, "Child Labor and Global Business: Lessons from the Apparel Industry in Bangladesh," *Journal of Asian Business* 15, no. 4 (1999): 81–91.

8. UNCRC Bangladesh Second Report, 72.

9. Ibid., especially pp. 71–72.

10. United Nations, Committee on the Rights of the Child, "Initial Reports of States Parties Due in 1992: Bangladesh. 07/12/95—Consideration of Reports Submitted by States Parties under Article 44 of the Convention [on the Rights of the Child]," CRC/C/3/Add.38, 7 December 1995, page 31 in electronic version. Hereafter referred to as UNCRC Bangladesh Initial Report. Available electronically via http://www.unhchr.ch/tbs/doc.nsf.

11. UNCRC Bangladesh Initial Report, pp. 23–33 in electronic version.

12. UNCRC Bangladesh Second Report, pp. 26, 31, 59, 74.

13. SAARC Third Ministerial Background Notes, 58.

14. For a critique of the abolitionist perspective, see Karl Hanson and Arne Vandaele. "Working Children and International Labor Law: A Critical Analysis," *International Journal of Children's Rights* 11, no. 1 (2003): 73–146. Hanson and Vandaele present an interesting analysis of the right to work as it relates to children; see especially pp. 90–97 and 125.

15. Ben White, "Children, Work and 'Child Labor': Changing Responses to the Employment of Children," *Development and Change* 25, no. 4 (October 1994): 849–78, especially p. 853.

16. Alam Rahman, interview by the author, New York City, 19 June 2004.

17. Lutfor Rahman Matin, director of BGMEA, quoted in Centre for Policy Dialogue, *Phasing Out of the Apparel Quota*, 83.

18. Sheena Crawford, *The Worst Forms of Child Labour: A Guide to Understanding and Using the New Convention* (London, UK: Department for International Development, Social Development Department, 2000).

19. U.S. Department of Labor, Bureau of International Labor Affairs, *Advancing the Campaign against Child Labor: Efforts at the Country Level* (Washington, DC: U.S. Department of Labor, International Labor Affairs Bureau, 2002), 30.

20. SAARC Third Ministerial Background Notes, 59.

21. Rijk van Haarlem, "BGMEA, ILO, UNICEF Child Labour Project Bangladesh: Case Study or 'Midterm Review,' " (Dhaka: ILO, July 1997).

22. Crawford, *Worst Forms of Child Labour*, 22.

23. Gayatri Chakravorty Spivak, *A Critique of Postcolonial Reason: Toward a History of the Vanishing Present* (Cambridge: Harvard University Press, 1999), 420. See pp. 414–21 for related discussion.

24. Quoted in Shahidul Alam, "Thank You, Mr. Harkin, Sir!" *New Internationalist*, no. 292 (July 1997), available electronically via http://www.newint.org/issue292/content .html.

25. UNICEF and ILO/IPEC, *Addressing Child Labour in the Bangladesh Garment Industry, 1995–2001: A Synthesis of UNICEF and ILO Evaluation Studies of the Bangladesh Garment Sector Projects* (New York and Geneva: UNICEF and ILO, August 2004). ILO/IPEC, *Combined Evaluation of the ILO/IPEC Garment Sector Projects as Part of the "Memorandum of Understanding" Framework with the Bangladesh Garment Manufacturers and Exporters Association* (Geneva: ILO/IPEC, April 2004). UNICEF, *Assessment of the Memorandum of Under-*

standing regarding Placement of Child Workers in School Programmes and Elimination of Child Labour in the Bangladesh Garment Industry, 1995–2001 (New York: UNICEF, 2004).

26. UNICEF and ILO/IPEC, *Addressing Child Labour in the Bangladesh Garment Industry*, 10.

27. Ibid., 19. See also ILO/IPEC, *Combined Evaluation of the ILO/IPEC Garment Sector Projects*, 19, 48.

28. UNICEF and ILO/IPEC, *Addressing Child Labour in the Bangladesh Garment Industry*, 12.

29. Ibid.

30. ILO/IPEC, *Combined Evaluation of the ILO/IPEC Garment Sector Projects*, 47.

31. Ibid., 14.

32. UNICEF and ILO/IPEC, *Addressing Child Labour in the Bangladesh Garment Industry*, 5.

33. For detail on the ILO's efforts in the area of child labor, see http://www.ilo.org/public/english/standards/ipec/. For detail on UNICEF's activities in relation to the Optional Protocols to the CRC, see http://www.unicef.org/crc/crc.htm.

34. Information on the Global March is available electronically via http://www.globalmarch.org.

35. Burns H. Weston, *Child Labor and Human Rights: Making Children Matter* (Boulder, CO: Lynne Rienner, 2005), especially chapters by Michael F. C. Bourdillon, David M. Post, Victor P. Karunan, and Ben White.

36. International Movement of Working Children, Dakar Declaration of March 1998, reprinted electronically and distributed via http://www.workingchild.org/prota2.htm.

37. Hanson and Vandaele, "Working Children and International Labor Law," particularly p. 133, nn. 2–6. Anthony Swift, "Let Us Work!" *New Internationalist*, no. 292 (July 1997), available electronically via http://www.newint.org/issue292/content.html.

38. Sarah C. White, "From the Politics of Poverty to the Politics of Identity? Child Rights and Working Children in Bangladesh," *Journal of International Development* 14 (2002): 725–35, especially pp. 725, 726, and 729.

39. Robert D. Putnam, "Diplomacy and Domestic Politics: The Logic of Two-Level Games," *International Organization* 42, no. 3 (summer 1988): 427–60.

40. White, "From the Politics of Poverty to the Politics of Identity?" 730, 733.

41. William Myers, personal email correspondence with the author, 20 August 2004.

42. Susan Bissell, "Young Garment Workers in Bangladesh: Raising the Rights Question," *Development* 44, no. 2 (2001): 75–80, especially pp. 76–77.

43. Ibid., 78–79. See also Naila Kabeer, *The Power to Choose: Bangladeshi Women and Labour Market Decisions in London and Dhaka* (London: Verso, 2000).

44. Ulrike Grote, Arnab Basu, Diana Weinhold, "Child Labor and the International Policy Debate,'" ZEF Discussion Papers on Development Policy, no. 1 (September 1998), Center for Development Research, Bonn, Germany, pp. 10–11, 31.

45. Shareen Hertel, "New Moves in Transnational Advocacy: Getting Labor and Economic Rights on the Agenda in Unexpected Ways," forthcoming in *Global Governance* 12, no. 3 (2006).

46. Lance Compa, "Free Trade, Fair Trade, and the Battle for Labor Rights," in *Rekindling the Movement: Labor's Quest for Relevance in the Twenty-first Century*, ed. Lowell Turner, Harry C. Katz, and Richard W. Hurd (Ithaca: Cornell University Press, 2001), 326.

47. Laurie J. Bremer, "Pregnancy Discrimination in Mexico's *Maquiladora* System: Mexico's Violation of Its Obligations under NAFTA and the NAALC," *NAFTA Law and Business Review of the Americas* 5, no. 4 (autumn 1999), 587.

48. Reka S. Koerner, "Pregnancy Discrimination in Mexico: Has Mexico Complied with the North American Agreement on Labor Cooperation?" *Texas Forum on Civil Liberties and Civil Rights* 4 (1998–99): 247.

49. Michelle Smith, "Potential Solutions to the Problem of Pregnancy Discrimination in *Maquiladoras* Operated by US Employers in Mexico," *Berkeley Women's Law Journal* 13 (1998): 221.

50. American Center for International Labor Solidarity/AFL-CIO. *Justice for All: The Struggle for Worker Rights in Mexico—A report by the Solidarity Center* (Washington, DC: AFL-CIO, 2003), 22. Hereafter, Solidarity Center, *Justice for All–Mexico.*

51. Solidarity Center, *Justice for All–Mexico*, 26.

52. Referenced in Linda Stevenson, "The Impact of Feminist Civil Society Movements and NGOs on Gender Policies in Mexico," paper presented at the annual meeting of the American Political Science Association, Chicago, 1–5 September 2004, 21.

53. Mónica Cavaría, "Necesario que las empresas privadas suspendan el examen de ingravidez," *Comunicación e información de la mujer*, 7 August 2001. Available electronically via http://www.cicam.org.mx/noticias/01ago. See also Nora Patricia Jara-López, "Foro nacional de consulta Proequidad: incertidumbres," *La Jornada*, 22 August 2001. Available electronically via http://www.jornada.unam.mx/2001/ago01/010822/038a1 cap.html. Nora Sandoval, "Las trabajadoras no son solo un útero, deben reconocerse sus derechos," *La Jornada*, 2 June 2002. Available electronically via http://www.jornada .unam.mx/2002/jun02/020603/articulos/46_trabajo.htm.

54. Solidarity Center, *Justice for All–Mexico*, 23.

55. Government of Mexico, Ley Federal Para Prevenir y Eliminar la Discriminación. Available electronically via http://www.diputados.gob.mx/leyinfo/pdf/262.pdf.

56. Solidarity Center, *Justice for All–Mexico*, 27.

57. Eduardo Díaz, quoted in John Nagel, "International Labor—Mexico's President Fox Signs New Anti-discrimination Law," *Daily Labor Report*, no. 112 (11 June 2003): A-4.

58. Stevenson, "Impact of Feminist Civil Society Movements and NGOs on Gender Policies in Mexico," 20.

59. Government of Mexico, Cámara de Diputados, LVII Legislatura, *Gaceta Parlamentaria*, 20 January 2003, no. 1172-1. Available electronically via http://gaceta.diputados .gob.mx/.

60. Human Rights Watch, "Mexico: Fox's Labor Reform Proposal Would Deal Serious Blow to Workers' Rights," letter to Mexico's Chamber of Deputies, 9 February 2005. Available electronically via http://hrw.org/english/docs/2005/02/09/mexico10156_txt .htm.

61. Ibid., 4. See also Government of Mexico, *Programa Nacional de Derechos Humanos* (Mexico City: Government of Mexico, December 2004), 166–67.

62. United Nations, Economic and Social Council, "Concluding Observations of the Committee on Economic, Social and Cultural Rights: Mexico 08/12/99," E/C.12/ 1/Add.41 (Concluding Observations/Comments), 8 December 1999, 5. Available electronically via http://www.unhchr.ch/tbs/doc.nsf/(Symbol)/E.C.12.1.ADD.41.En ?Opendocument.

63. Smith, "Potential Solutions," 220. For related discussion of the 9701 case, see pp. 219–21.

64. Solidarity Center, *Justice for All–Mexico*, 41.

65. Nicole L. Grimm, "The North American Agreement on Labor Cooperation and Its Effects on Women Working in Mexican *Maquiladoras*," *American University Law Review* 48, no. 1 (October 1998): 180–224. P. 43 of online version, available electronically via http:// www.wcl.american.edu/journal/lawrev/48/pdf/grimm.pdf.

66. Bremer, "Pregnancy Discrimination," 573 and 575.

67. Peter Gourevitch, "The Second Image Reversed: The International Sources of Domestic Politics," *International Organization* 32, no. 4 (autumn 1978): 881–911.

68. Linda Stevenson, "Confronting Gender Discrimination in the Mexican Workplace:

Women and Labor Facing NAFTA with Transnational Contention," *Women and Politics* 26, no. 1 (2004): 71–97.

69. Ibid., 88.

70. Subsequent work by HRW on pregnancy screening in Latin America has included a report on conditions in Guatemala, *From the Household to the Factory: Sex Discrimination in the Guatemala Labor Force* (New York: Human Rights Watch, 2002). As is evident from the title, the report remains focused on issues of discrimination.

71. Stevenson, "Impact of Feminist Civil Society Movements and NGOs on Gender Policies in Mexico," 12–13. Stevenson credits Amy Mazur with developing several of the core concepts in this model, in Amy Mazur, *Gender Bias and the State: Symbolic Reform at Work in Fifth Republic France* (Pittsburgh: University of Pittsburgh Press, 1995).

72. Stevenson, "Impact of Feminist Civil Society Movements and NGOs on Gender Policies in Mexico," 14.

73. United Nations, *Report of the Committee on the Elimination of Discrimination against Women* (eighteenth and nineteenth sessions), General Assembly, Official Records, 53rd session, supplement no. 38 (A/53/38/Rev.1).

74. Veronica Schild, " 'Gender Equity' without Social Justice: Women's Rights in the Neoliberal Age," *NACLA Report on the Americas* 34, no. 1 (July/August 2000): 25–28, particularly p. 28. Alison Brysk, "Globalization: The Double-Edged Sword," *NACLA Report on the Americas* 34, no. 1 (July/August 2000): 29–33, particularly p. 31.

75. Examples of such codes include Social Accountability 8000 (SA8000) and the Workplace Code of Conduct of the Fair Labor Association, both included in Deborah Leipziger, *The Corporate Responsibility Code Book* (Sheffield, UK: Greenleaf, November 2003).

6. Conclusion

1. Clifford Bob, *The Marketing of Rebellion: Insurgents, Media, and International Activism* (Cambridge: Cambridge University Press, 2005).

2. Bread for the World, "Proclaim Jubilee: Break the Chains of Debt," *1999 Offering of Letters Kit* (Washington, DC: BFW, 1999), 7–13. United Nations Nongovernmental Liaison Service, "Jubilee South-South Summit," *Go Between* 78 (December 1999–January 2000): 19. Josh Busby, "Bono Made Jesse Helms Cry: International Norms Take-Up and the Jubilee 2000 Campaign for Debt Relief," Paper presented at the annual meeting of the American Political Science Association, Philadelphia, PA, 28–31 August 2003. Available electronically via http://www.georgetown.edu/users/busbyj/debt.pdf.

3. For details on the work of Jubilee South, see http://www.jubileesouth.org/ and for detail on Jubilee-USA (as an example of Jubilee North), see http://www.jubileeusa.org/jubilee.cgi.

4. E. R. Shipp, "Rosa Parks, 92, Founding Symbol of Civil Rights Movement, Dies," *New York Times*, 25 October 2005, A1.

5. I am indebted to Dr. Evelyn M. Simien for suggestions of related literature, including Belinda Robnett, *How Long? How Long? African-American Women in the Struggle for Civil Rights* (Oxford: Oxford University Press, 2000). Belinda Robnett, "African-American Women in the Civil Rights Movement, 1954–1965: Gender, Leadership, and Micromobilization," *American Journal of Sociology* 101, no. 6 (May 1996): 1661–93. Benita Roth, *Separate Roads to Feminism: Black, Chicana, and White Feminist Movements in America's Second Wave* (Cambridge: Cambridge University Press, 2004).

6. Margaret Keck and Kathryn Sikkink, "Transnational Advocacy Networks in International and Regional Politics," *International Social Science Journal* 159 (1999): 92, 100.

Appendix 3

1. References to the Federal Labor Law can be found in Mireya Scarone-Adarga, "Prohibido embarazarse: los derechos reproductivos de las trabajadoras en Hermosillo" (B.A. thesis, Universidad de Sonora, 2001), 45–46; CIESEX, MUTUAC-MAS, GIRE, "Propuestas de Reforma a la Ley Federal del Trabajo para desalentar la práctica del despido por embarazo y los exámenes de no gravidez," 2–7, undated photocopy on file with the author; Human Rights Watch, *No Guarantees: Sex Discrimination in Mexico's Maquiladora Sector* (New York: Human Rights Watch, 1996),35–36; and in CIESEX, DIVERSA, MUTUAC-MAS, GIRE, and UTM, "Campaña para desalentar la práctica del despido por maternidad y el exámen de no embarazo," undated fact sheet, photocopy on file with the author.

2. References to the Constitution of Mexico can be found in Scarone-Adarga, "Prohibido embarazarse: los derechos reproductivos de las trabajadoras en Hermosillo," 59, 45.

3. For full text of the ILO conventions that follow, consult the ILO website http:// ilolex.ilo.ch:1567/english/docs/convdisp.htm. ILO recommendations are listed separately under http://ilolex.ilo.ch:1567/english/docs/recdisp.htm. References to adoption of ILO conventions and/or recommendations can be found in Scarone-Adarga, "Prohibido embarazarse: los derechos reproductivos de las trabajadoras en Hermosillo," 45, and throughout campaign literature, for example, CIESEX and DIVERSA, "Comunicado de Prensa," 5 March 1998.

4. References to UN conventions as benchmarks can be found in: Scarone-Adarga, "Prohibido embarazarse: los derechos reproductivos de las trabajadoras en Hermosillo," 99. Reference to CEDAW is widespread throughout campaign literature, for example, in Yolanda Ramírez-León, "La Conciliación entre Maternidad y Trabajo," unpublished manuscript, March 1999, on file with the author.

References

Abdullah, Abu A. "Social Change and 'Modernization.'" In *Bangladesh: Promise and Performance*, ed. Rounaq Jahan, 129–47. London: Zed Books, 2001.

"Activists blast US bill on child labor." United Press International, 8 August 1993.

Alam, Shahidul. "Thank You, Mr. Harkin, Sir!" *New Internationalist*, no. 292 (July 1997). Available electronically via http://www.newint.org/issue292/content.html.

Alcántara, Liliana. "Se unen legisladoras al apoyo a trabajadoras embarazadas." *El Universal*, 22 October 1998.

Alston, Philip. "The Commission on Human Rights." In *The United Nations and Human Rights: A Critical Appraisal*, ed. Alston, 126–210. Oxford: Clarendon Press, 1992.

American Center for International Labor Solidarity/American Federation of Labor and Congress of Industrial Organizations (AFL-CIO). *Justice for All: The Struggle for Worker Rights in Mexico—A Report by the Solidarity Center*. Washington, DC: AFL-CIO, 2003.

Amin, Sajeda, and Cynthia B. Lloyd. "Women's Lives and Rapid Fertility Decline: Some Lessons from Bangladesh and Egypt." Population Council Working Papers series, no. 117. New York: Population Council, 1998.

Anner, Mark. "The International Trade Union Campaign for Core Labor Standards in the WTO." *Working USA* 5, no. 1 (summer 2001): 43–63.

Apodaca, Clair. "Measuring Women's Economic and Social Rights Achievement." *Human Rights Quarterly* 20, no. 1 (1998): 139–72.

Association for Women's Rights in Development (AWID). "The International Covenant on Economic, Social and Cultural Rights." *Women's Rights and Economic Change—Facts and Issues* 3 (August 2002): 1–8.

Balikrishnan, Radhika. *The Hidden Assembly Line: Gender Dynamics of Subcontracted Work in a Global Economy*. Bloomfield, CT: Kumarian Press, 2002.

Baxi, Upendra. "The Development of the Right to Development." In *Human Rights:*

New Dimensions and Challenges, ed. Janusz Symonides, 99–116. Brookfield, MA: Ashgate, 1998.

Begum, Najmir Nur. "Women in Ready-Made Garment Industries: Issues and Concerns." Unpublished working paper commissioned by the Ministry of Textiles, Textile Strategic Management Unit. Dhaka: Government of Bangladesh, 1997.

"BGMEA Warns Members of Dire Consequences of Employing Children." *Morning Sun*, 31 December 1992.

Bhattacharya, Debapriya. "International Trade, Social Labelling and Developing Countries: The Case of Bangladesh's Garments Export and Use of Child Labor." In *Annuaire Suisse-Tiers Monde*, ed. J. Forster, 215–38. Geneva: University Institute of Developing Studies, 1996.

Bissell, Susan. "Young Garment Workers in Bangladesh: Raising the Rights Question." *Development* 44, no. 2 (2001): 75–80.

Bob, Clifford. "Constructing New Human Rights Norms: A Theoretical Framework." Paper presented at the annual meeting of the International Studies Association, Montreal, Canada, 17–20 March 2004.

———. *The Marketing of Rebellion: Insurgents, Media and International Activism*. Cambridge: Cambridge University Press, 2005.

———. "Marketing Rebellion: Insurgent Groups, International Media, and NGO Support." *International Politics* 38 (September 2001): 311–34.

———. "Merchants of Morality." *Foreign Policy* 129 (March/April 2002): 36–45.

Bonifaz-Alonso, Leticia. *El problema de la eficacia en el derecho*. Mexico City: Editorial Porrúa, 1993.

Boyden, Jo, Birgitta Ling, and William Myers. *What Works for Working Children*. Stockholm: Radda Barnen 1998.

Bread for the World. "Proclaim Jubilee: Break the Chains of Debt." *1999 Offering of Letters Kit*. Washington, DC: BFW, 1999.

Bremer, Laurie J. "Pregnancy Discrimination in Mexico's *Maquiladora* System: Mexico's Violation of Its Obligations under NAFTA and the NAALC." *NAFTA Law and Business Review of the Americas* 5, no. 4 (autumn 1999): 567–88.

Broad, Robin, ed. *Global Backlash: Citizen Initiatives for a Just World Economy*. Lanham, MD: Rowman and Littlefield, 2002.

Brooks, Ethel. "The Consumer's New Clothes: Global Protest, the New International Division of Labor, and Women's Work in the Garment Industry." Ph.D. diss., New York University, 2000.

Brysk, Alison. "Globalization: The Double-Edged Sword." *NACLA Report on the Americas* 34, no. 1 (July/August 2000): 29–33.

Bunch, Charlotte. *Demanding Accountability: The Global Campaign and Vienna Tribunal for Women's Human Rights*. New Brunswick, NJ: Center for Women's Global Leadership, Douglass College, Rutgers University; New York: United Nations Development Fund for Women, 1994.

Burgoon, Brian. "Uncertain Coalitions and the Political Economy of Fair Trade: Labor Rights Linkage in Domestic and International Politics." Paper presented at the annual meeting of the International Studies Association, Chicago, IL, 20–24 February 2001.

Busby, Josh. "Bono Made Jesse Helms Cry: International Norms Take-Up and the Jubilee 2000 Campaign for Debt Relief." Paper presented at the annual meeting of the American Political Science Association, Philadelphia, PA, 28–31 August 2003. Available electronically via http://www.georgetown.edu/users/busbyj/debt.pdf.

Candland, Christopher. "How Do International Norms Evolve? Debate and Action on International Labor Standards." Paper presented at the annual meeting of the American Political Science Association, Washington, DC, 28–31 August 1997.

Carter, Miguel. "Ideal Interest Mobilization: Explaining the Formation of Brazil's Landless Social Movement." Ph.D. diss., Columbia University, 2002.

Casa de la Mujer–Hermosillo. "8 de Marzo, Día internacional de la mujer." Undated photocopy on file with the author.

——. "Mujeres trabajadoras en Sonora: Algunas consideraciones a tomarse en cuenta para elaborar un pliego petitorio de trabajadoras en el estado." Undated photocopy on file with the author.

Cassidy, John. "Master of Disaster." *New Yorker*, 15 July 2000, 82–86.

Cavaría, Mónica. "Necesario que las empresas privadas suspendan el exámen de ingravidez." *Comunicación e información de la mujer*, 7 August 2001. Available electronically via http://www.cicam.org.mx/noticias/01ago.

Centre for Policy Dialogue. *Phasing Out of the Apparel Quota: Addressing Livelihood Concerns in Bangladesh*. Dhaka, Bangladesh: University Press, 2003.

Centro de Investigación y Estudio de la Sexualidad (CIESEX) and DIVERSA. "Comunicado de Prensa." CIESEX-DIVERSA/COM002, Mexico City, 5 March 1998.

Centro de Investigación y Estudio de la Sexualidad (CIESEX), DIVERSA, Mujeres Trabajadoras Unidas, AC/Mujeres en Acción Sindical (MUTUAC/MAS), Grupo de Información en Reproducción Elegida (GIRE), and Unión de Trabajadoras Mexicanas (UTM). "Campaña para desalentar la práctica del despido por maternidad y el exámen de no embarazo." Undated fact sheet on file with the author.

Centro de Investigación y Estudio de la Sexualidad (CIESEX), Mujeres Trabajadoras Unidas, AC/Mujeres en Acción Sindical (MUTUAC/MAS), and Grupo de Información en Reproducción Elegida (GIRE). "Propuestas de reforma a la Ley Federal del Trabajo para desalentar la práctica del despido por embarazo y los exámenes de no gravidez." Undated photocopy on file with the author.

Cervantes, Erika. "Nueva identidad: los derechos de las mujeres al interior de las familias." Unpublished document, February 1998. Reprinted in Casa de la Mujer–Hermosillo, "8 de Marzo, Día internacional de la mujer." Undated photocopy on file with the author.

Cervantes, Jesús. "Crearán un tribunal para denunciar despidos por embarazo." *La Jornada*, 6 March 1998.

Chapman, Audrey R. "A 'Violations Approach' for Monitoring the International Covenant on Economic, Social and Cultural Rights." *Human Rights Quarterly* 18, no. 1 (1996): 23–66.

Chawla, Nilima. *In Search of the Best Interests of the Child: A First Step towards Eliminating Child Labour in the Bangladesh Garment Industry*. Dhaka: UNICEF, October 1996.

Cheah, Pheng. "Posit(ion)ing Human Rights in the Current Global Conjuncture." *Public Culture* 9 (1997): 233–66.

"Child Labor and International Law." *Dainik Bangla*, 8 August 1993.

Chowdhury, Sumaira. "When Motives Matter: The 1993 Child Labor Deterrence Act and the Memorandum of Understanding." Undergraduate thesis, Wellesley College, 1998.

Clark, Ann Marie, Elisabeth J. Friedman, and Kathryn Hochstetler. "The Sovereign Limits of Global Civil Society: A Comparison of NGO Participation in UN World Conferences on the Environment, Human Rights, and Women." *World Politics* 51, no. 1 (October 1988): 1–25.

Coalition for Justice in the Maquiladoras. *Guía para la Ley Federal del Trabajo, parte 1 y parte 2*. San Antonio, TX: Coalition for Justice in the Maquiladoras, 1997.

Columbia University, Center for the Study of Human Rights. *Twenty-five Human Rights Documents*. New York: Columbia University, 1994.

——. *Woman and Human Rights: The Basic Documents*. New York: Columbia University, 1996.

Compa, Lance. "Free Trade, Fair Trade, and the Battle for Labor Rights." In *Rekindling the Movement: Labor's Quest for Relevance in the Twenty-first Century*, ed. Lowell Turner, Harry C. Katz, and Richard W. Hurd, 314–38. Ithaca: Cornell University Press, 2001.

——. "The Promise and Perils of 'Core' Labor Rights in Global Trade and Investment." Paper presented at Human Rights for the Twenty-First Century conference, The Graduate Center, City University of New York, New York City, 17–18 November 2000.

Consorcio para el Diálogo Parlamentario y la Equidad. "La equidad de género en la LVII legislatura." In *Agenda Afirmativa*. Undated pamphlet on file with the author

Cortright, David, and George Lopez. "Assessing Smart Sanctions: Lessons from the 1990s," in *Smart Sanctions: Targeting Economic Statecraft*, ed. David Cortright and George Lopez, 1–22. Lanham, MD: Rowman and Littlefield, 2002.

Crawford, Neta C., and Audie Klotz, eds. *How Sanctions Work: Lessons from South Africa*. New York: St. Martin's Press, 1999.

Crawford, Sheena. *The Worst Forms of Child Labour: A Guide to Understanding and Using the New Convention*. London, UK: Department for International Development, Social Development Department, 2000.

Cronin, Ciaran, and Pablo DeGreiff, eds. *Transnational Politics and Deliberative Democracy*. Cambridge: MIT Press, 2002.

Cuevas, Leticia R., with Kathlene McDonald. "Analysis of Issues Raised in Submission 9701, Gender Discrimination and Pregnancy Based Discrimination." Unpublished manuscript, December 1997. Available electronically via http://www.dol.gov/ILAB/media/reports/nao/9701analysis.htm.

Delap, Emily. "Economic and Cultural Forces in the Child Labour Debate: Evidence from Urban Bangladesh." *Journal of Development Studies* 37, no. 4 (April 2001): 1–22.

The Economist. *Pocket World in Figures: 2002 Edition*. London: Profile Books, 2002.

Edwards, Michael, and John Gaventa, eds. *Global Citizen Action*. Boulder, CO: Lynne Rienner, 2001.

Elster, Jon. *Alchemies of the Mind: Rationality and the Emotions*. Cambridge: Cambridge University Press, 1999.

Evans, Peter. "Fighting Marginalization with Transnational Networks: Counter-Hegemonic Globalization." *Contemporary Sociology* 29, no. 1 (January 2000): 230–41.

Farha, Leilani. "Women's Rights and Economics: How Can We Promote Women's Economic, Social and Cultural Rights Internationally?" *AWID News* 4, no. 3 (autumn 2000): 1.

Fernández, Berta. "Piden eliminar la discriminación que sufren las mujeres embarazadas en sus empleos." *El Universal*, 6 March 1998.

Fernández-Kelly, María Patricia. *For We Are Sold, I and My People: Women and Industry in Mexico's Frontier*. Albany, NY: State University of New York Press, 1983.

Finnemore, Martha, and Kathryn Sikkink. "International Norm Dynamics and Political Change." *International Organization* 52, no. 4 (autumn 1998): 887–917.

Florini, Ann M., ed. *The Third Force: The Rise of Transnational Civil Society*. Washington, DC: Brookings Institution Press, 2000.

Fox, Jonathan. "Assessing Bi-national Civil Society Coalitions: Lessons from the US-Mexico Experience." Working paper no. 26, April 2000. Santa Cruz, CA: University of California–Santa Cruz.

———. "Lessons from Mexico-US Civil Society Coalitions," in *Cross Border Dialogues: US-Mexico Social Movement Networking*, ed. David Brooks and Jonathan Fox, 341–418. La Jolla, CA: Center for US-Mexican Studies, University of California–San Diego, 2002.

———. "State-Society Relations in Mexico: Historical Legacies and Contemporary Trends." *Latin American Research Review* 35, no. 2 (2000): 183–203.

Friedman, Monroe. "Grassroots Groups Confront the Corporation: Contemporary Strategies in Historical Perspective." *Journal of Social Issues* 52, no. 1 (spring 1996): 153–68.

García, Rubén. "Crear tribunal contra la marginación a mujeres, piden ONGs." *El Nacional*, 6 March 1998.

García-Pelayo y Gross, Román. *Pequeño Larousse ilustrado*. Barcelona: Ediciones Larousse, 1989.

"Género: Avances de la igualdad." *La Jornada*, 22 May 1999.

George, Alexander, and Tim McKeown. "Case Studies and Theories of Organizational Decisionmaking." *Advances in International Information Processing* 2 (1985): 21–58.

Gerring, John. *Case Study Research: Principles and Practices*. Cambridge: Cambridge University Press, forthcoming.

Giddens, Anthony. *The Constitution of Society: Outline of the Theory of Structuration*. Cambridge: Cambridge University Press, 1984.

———. *New Rules of Sociological Method: A Positive Critique of Interpretative Sociologies*. Stanford: Stanford University Press, 1993.

Giugni, Marco. *How Social Movements Matter*. Minneapolis: University of Minnesota Press, 1999.

Glut, Timothy A. "Changing the Approach to Ending Child Labor: An International Solution to an International Problem." *Vanderbilt Journal of Transnational Law* 28 (1995): 1203–44.

González-Baz, Aureliano. "Manufacturing in Mexico: The Mexican In-Bond (*Maquila*) Program." Available electronically via http://www.udel.edu/leipzig/texts2/vox128.htm.

Gourevitch, Peter. "The Second Image Reversed: The International Sources of Domestic Politics." *International Organization* 32, 4 (autumn 1978): 881–911.

Government of Mexico. *Programa Nacional de Derechos Humanos*. Mexico City: Government of Mexico, December 2004.

Government of Mexico, Cámara de Diputados, LVII Legislatura. *Gaceta Parlamentaria*, 20 January 2003, no. 1172-1. Available electronically via http://gaceta.diputados.gob.mx/.

Government of Mexico, Procuraduría de los Derechos Humanos y Protección Ciudadana del Estado de Baja California. "Mensaje del Procurador de Los Derechos Humanos, C. Raúl Ramírez Baena: La larga lucha por los Derechos Sociales." *Gaceta*, January–September 2001, 4–5.

Government of Mexico, Secretaría del Trabajo y Previsión Social (Mexicali, Baja California). "Reformas a la Ley del Seguro Social: Programa de Lactancia Corporativa y Hostigamiento Sexual." May 2001. Photocopy on file with the author.

Green, Maria. "What We Talk About When We Talk About Indicators: Current Approaches to Human Rights Measurement." *Human Rights Quarterly* 23 (2001): 1062–97.

Green, Paula L. "Child Labor Coalition May Seek Bangladesh Boycott." *Journal of Commerce*, 15 May 1995.

Grewal, Inderpal. " 'Women's Rights as Human Rights': Feminist Practices, Global Feminism, and Human Rights Regimes in Transnationality." *Citizenship Studies* 3, no. 3 (1999): 337–54.

Grimm, Nicole L., "The North American Agreement on Labor Cooperation and Its Effects on Women Working in Mexican *Maquiladoras*." *American University Law Review* 48, no. 1 (October 1998): 180–224.

Grote, Ulrike, Arnab Basu, and Diana Weinhold. "Child Labor and the International Policy Debate.' " ZEF Discussion Papers on Development Policy, no. 1 (September 1998). Bonn, Germany, Center for Development Research.

Haas, Richard N., ed. *Economic Sanctions and American Diplomacy*. New York: Council on Foreign Relations, distributed by Brookings Institution Press, 1998.

Hamilton, Nora. *The Limits of State Autonomy: Post-Revolutionary Mexico*. Princeton: Princeton University Press, 1982.

Hanson, Karl, and Arne Vandaele. "Working Children and International Labor Law: A Critical Analysis." *International Journal of Children's Rights* 11, no. 1 (2003): 73–146.

Harvey, Pharis. "Historic Breakthrough for Bangladesh Kids Endangered by Industry Inaction." *Worker Rights News*, no. 12 (August 1995): 1, 5, 6.

——. "Press Statement: Labor Rights Fund Urges Passage of Re-introduced International Child Labor Deterrence Act." International Labor Rights Fund, 8 March 1993. Photocopy on file with the author.

Henneberger, Melinda. "Outcry Grows over Police Use of Force in Genoa." *New York Times*, 8 August 2001.

Herrera-Beltrán, Claudia. "Eliminan el certificado de ingravidez para mujeres en educación." *La Jornada*, 21 May 1999.

Hertel, Shareen. "New Moves in Transnational Advocacy: Getting Labor and Economic Rights on the Agenda in Unexpected Ways." *Global Governance* 12, no. 3 (2006).

——. "What Was All the Shouting About? Strategic Bargaining and Protest at the WTO Third Ministerial (Seattle, Washington, USA—November 1999)." *Human Rights Review* 6, no. 3 (April–June 2005): 102–18.

——. "Why Bother? Measuring Economic Rights—The Research Agenda." *International Studies Perspectives* 7, no. 3 (forthcoming).

Human Rights Watch. *From the Household to the Factory: Sex Discrimination in the Guatemala Labor Force*. New York: Human Rights Watch, 2002.

——. *A Job or Your Rights: Continued Sex Discrimination in Mexico's Maquiladora Sector*. New York: Human Rights Watch, 1998.

——. "Mexico: Fox's Labor Reform Proposal Would Deal Serious Blow to Workers' Rights." Letter to Mexico's Chamber of Deputies, 9 February 2005. Available electronically via http://hrw.org/english/docs/2005/02/09/mexico10156_txt.htm.

——. *No Guarantees: Sex Discrimination in Mexico's Maquiladora Sector*. New York: Human Rights Watch, 1996.

——. *Trading Away Rights: The Unfulfilled Promise of NAFTA's Labor Side Agreement*, vol. 13, no. 2 B (April 2001).

——. *World Report 2000*. New York: Human Rights Watch, 2000.

Hunt, Paul. *Reclaiming Social Rights: International and Comparative Perspectives*. Brookfield, VT: Dartmouth Publishing Group, 1996.

International Labour Organization (ILO). "A Future without Child Labour: Global Report under the Follow-up to the ILO Declaration on Fundamental Principles and Rights at Work." Prepared for the International Labour Conference, 90th session, 2002, Report I-B, Geneva.

International Labour Organization (ILO) International Programme on the Elimination of Child Labour. "BGMEA, ILO, UNICEF Child Labor Project Bangladesh: Case Study or 'Midterm' Review." Internal working paper prepared by Rijk van Haarlem, July 1997, on file with the author.

——. *Combined Evaluation of the ILO/IPEC Garment Sector Projects as Part of the 'Memorandum of Understanding' Framework with the Bangladesh Garment Manufacturers and Exporters Association*. Geneva: ILO/IPEC, April 2004.

——. *The Memorandum of Understanding (MOU) between BGMEA, ILO, and UNICEF: A "Quick Reference" Pamphlet*. Dhaka, Bangladesh: ILO/IPEC, October 1996.

Jahan, Rounaq, ed. *Bangladesh: Promise and Performance*. London: Zed Books, 2001.

Jara-López, Nora Patricia. "Foro nacional de consulta Proequidad: incertidumbres." *La Jornada*, 22 August 2001. Available electronically via http://www.jornada.unam.mx/2001/ago01/010822/038a1cap.html.

Judkins, Benjamin N. "Economic Statecraft and Regime Type: Transparency, Credibility, and Conflict Resolution." Paper presented at the annual meeting of the International Studies Association, Portland, Oregon, 25 February–1 March 2003. Available electronically via http://www.isanet.org/portlandarchive/judkins.html.

Kabeer, Naila. *The Power to Choose: Bangladeshi Women and Labour Market Decisions in London and Dhaka*. London: Verso, 2000.

Kamel, Rachel, and Anya Hoffman, eds. *The Maquiladora Reader: Cross-Border Organizing since NAFTA*. Philadelphia: American Friends Service Committee, 1999.

Katzenstein, Peter J., ed. *The Culture of National Security: Norms and Identity in World Politics*. New York: Columbia University Press, 1996.

Keck, Margaret, and Kathryn Sikkink. *Activists Beyond Borders: Transnational Advocacy Networks in International Politics*. Ithaca: Cornell University Press, 1998.

——. "Transnational Advocacy Networks in International and Regional Politics." *International Social Science Journal* 159 (1999): 89–101.

——. "Transnational Advocacy Networks in Movement Society." In *The Social Movement Society: Contentious Politics for a New Century*, ed. David S. Meyer and Sidney Tarrow, 217–62. Lanham, MD: Rowman and Littlefield, 1998.

Klein, Jill Gabrielle, Craig N. Smith, and Andrew John. "Why We Boycott: Consumer Motivations for Boycott Participation." *Journal of Marketing* 68, no. 3 (2003): 92–110.

Klotz, Audie. *Norms in International Relations: The Struggle against Apartheid*. Ithaca: Cornell University Press, 1995.

Koch, Ida. "Social Rights as Components in the Civil Right to Personal Liberty: Another Step Forward in the Integrated Human Rights Approach?" *Netherlands Quarterly of Human Rights* 20, no. 1 (2002): 29–51.

Kochanek, Stanley A. "The Growing Commercialization of Power." In *Bangladesh: Promise and Performance*, ed. Rounaq Jahan, 149–79. London: Zed Books, 2001.

Koerner, Reka S. "Pregnancy Discrimination in Mexico: Has Mexico Complied with the North American Agreement on Labor Cooperation?" *Texas Forum on Civil Liberties and Civil Rights* 4 (1998–99): 235–64.

Kowert, Paul and Jeffrey Legro. "Norms, Identity and Their Limits: A Theoretical Reprise." In *The Culture of National Security: Norms and Identity in World Politics*, ed. Peter J. Katzenstein, 451–97. New York: Columbia University Press, 1996.

Krasner, Stephen D. "Structural Causes and Regime Consequences: Regimes as Intervening Variables." In *International Regimes*, ed. Krasner, 1–21. Ithaca: Cornell University Press, 1983.

Kunnemann, Rolf. "A Coherent Approach to Human Rights." *Human Rights Quarterly* 17, no. 2 (1995): 323–42.

Leary, Virginia. "Lessons from the Experience of the International Labour Organisation." In *The United Nations and Human Rights: A Critical Appraisal*, ed. Philip Alston, 580–619. Oxford: Clarendon Press, 1992.

——. "The Paradox of Workers' Rights as Human Rights." In *Human Rights, Labor Rights, and International Trade*, ed. Lance Compa and Stephen Diamond, 22–47. Philadelphia: University of Pennsylvania Press, 1996.

Leipziger, Deborah. *The Corporate Responsibility Code Book*. Sheffield, UK: Greenleaf, November 2003.

Lichbach, Mark I., and Alan S. Zuckerman, eds. *Comparative Politics: Rationality, Culture and Structure*. Cambridge: Cambridge University Press, 1997.

Liton, Nur Khan. "Harkin's Law: More Harm Than Good." *Dhaka Courier*, 18 September 1993. Reprinted in Ain-O-Salish Kendra (ASK), *Rights and Realities*. Dhaka: ASK, September 1997.

Mahoney, James. "Beyond Correlational Analysis: Recent Innovations in Theory and Method." *Sociological Forum* 16, no. 3 (September 2001): 575–93.

"Las maquiladoras, espejismo ante el desempleo." *Diario Yucatán*, 3 March 1999.

Martínez, Fabiola. "Convocan a foro de conciliación entre la maternidad y el trabajo." *La Jornada*, 22 October 1998.

Mazhar, Farhad. "Mr. Harkin's Talk of 'Human Rights'—or Scripture from the Mouth of Satan." *Ajker Kagoj*, 1993. Photocopy on file with the author.

Mazur, Amy. *Gender Bias and the State: Symbolic Reform at Work in Fifth Republic France*. Pittsburgh: University of Pittsburgh Press, 1995.

McAdam, Doug, John McCarthy, and Mayer Zald, eds. *Comparative Perspectives on Social Movements: Political Opportunities, Mobilizing Structures, and Cultural Framing*. New York: Cambridge University Press, 1996.

McAdam, Doug, Sidney Tarrow, and Charles Tilly. *Dynamics of Contention*. Cambridge: Cambridge University Press, 2001.

Moody, Kim. *Workers in a Lean World: Unions in the International Economy*. New York: Verso Books, 1997.

Mujeres Trabajadoras Unidas, AC/Mujeres en Acción Sindical (MUTUAC/MAS), DIVERSAS, Centro de Investigación y Estudio de la Sexualidad (CIESEX), Equidad y Género, and Grupo de Información en Reproducción Elegida (GIRE). *Cartilla: Maternidad y Trabajo—Pueden conciliarse?* Undated pamphlet on file with the author.

——. "Informe narrativo de la campaña: la Conciliación entre Maternidad y Trabajo." Unpublished report, 1998, on file with the author.

——. "Resúmen de casos presentados en el marco del Tribunal de Conciliación entre la Maternidad y el Trabajo." Unpublished collection of testimony, presented at the Tribunal on Reconciling Maternity and Work, Mexico City, 22 October 1998, on file with the author.

Munck, Ronaldo, and Peter Waterman, eds. *Labor Worldwide in an Era of Globalization*. New York: St. Martin's Press, 1999.

Nagel, John. "International Labor—Mexico's President Fox Signs New Anti-Discrimination Law." *Daily Labor Report*, no. 112 (11 June 2003): A-4.

National Consumers League. "Consumer Boycott Spurs Responsible End to Child Labor." *NCL Bulletin* 57, no. 3 (May-June-July 1995): 1, 9.

"New Challenge for Garments Industry." *Daily Star*, 2 January 1993.

Nielsen, Michael E. "The Politics of Corporate Responsibility and Child Labour in the Bangladeshi Garment Industry." *International Affairs* 81, no. 3 (May 2005): 559–81.

Ochoa, Teresa. "Denuncian discriminación," *Reforma*, 3 March 1999.

"On the Question of Child Labor." *Janakantha*, 5 August 1993.

"The Other Government in Bangladesh." *Economist*, 25 July 1998, 42.

Putnam, Robert D. "Diplomacy and Domestic Politics: The Logic of Two-Level Games." *International Organization* 42, no. 3 (summer 1988): 427–60.

Quddus, Munir. "Child Labor and Global Business: Lessons from the Apparel Industry in Bangladesh." *Journal of Asian Business* 15, no. 4 (1999): 81–91.

Quintero-Ramírez, Cirila. "Participación femenina en las maquiladoras: reconsideraciones y nuevas hipóteses." Paper presented at the First Congress on Women's Studies in the North of Mexico and South of the United States, El Colegio de la Frontera Norte, Matamoros Campus, Monterrey, Nuevo León, 23–25 October 1997.

Rahman, Mohammad M., Rasheda Khanan, and Nur Uddin Absar. "Child Labor in Bangladesh: A Critical Appraisal of Harkin's Bill and the MOU-Type Schooling Program." *Journal of Economic Issues* 1, no. 33 (December 1999): 874–1003.

Rahman, Wahidur. "Paper for Roundtable Conference on Child Labor." Prepared for a meeting hosted by the International Labour Organization, International Programme on Child Labour, Dhaka, Bangladesh. Undated photocopy on file with the author.

Ramírez-Leon, Yolanda. "La Conciliación entre Maternidad y Trabajo." Unpublished manuscript, March 1999, on file with the author.

Risse, Thomas, Stephen C. Ropp, and Kathryn Sikkink, eds. *The Power of Human Rights: International Norms and Domestic Change*. Cambridge: Cambridge University Press, 1999.

Robnett, Belinda. "African-American Women in the Civil Rights Movement, 1954–1965: Gender, Leadership, and Micromobilization." *American Journal of Sociology* 101, no. 6 (May 1996): 1661–93.

——. *How Long? How Long? African-American Women in the Struggle for Civil Rights*. Oxford: Oxford University Press, 2000.

Rosenbaum, Ruth. *Making the Invisible Visible: A Study of Purchasing Power of Maquila Workers in Mexico 2000*. Hartford, CT: Center for Reflection, Education and Action, 2000.

Ross, Andrew, ed. *No Sweat: Fashion, Free Trade and the Rights of Garment Workers*. London: Verso, 1997.

Roth, Benita. *Separate Roads to Feminism: Black, Chicana, and White Feminist Movements in America's Second Wave*. Cambridge: Cambridge University Press, 2004.

Salazar, Miguel. "Denuncian aplicación de exámen de no gravidez en mujeres recién contratadas." *El Sol de México*, 22 October 1998.

Sandoval, Nora. "Las trabajadoras no son solo un útero, deben reconocerse sus derechos." *La Jornada*, 2 June 2002. Available electronically via http://www.jornada.unam.mx/2002/jun02/020603/articulos/46_trabajo.htm.

Scarone-Adarga, Mireya. "Prohibido embarazarse: los derechos reproductivos de las trabajadoras en Hermosillo." B.A. thesis, Universidad de Sonora, 2001.

Schild, Veronica. " 'Gender Equity' without Social Justice: Women's Rights in the

Neoliberal Age." *NACLA Report on the Americas* 34, no. 1 (July/August 2000): 25–28.

Scott, James C. *Domination and the Arts of Resistance: Hidden Transcripts*. New Haven, CT: Yale University Press, 1990.

Sen, Binayak. "Growth, Poverty and Human Development." In *Bangladesh: Promise and Performance*, ed. Rounaq Jahan, 267–308. London: Zed Books, 2001.

Shipp, E. R. "Rosa Parks, 92, Founding Symbol of Civil Rights Movement, Dies." *New York Times*, 25 October 2005, A1.

Smith, Jackie. "Globalizing Resistance: The Battle of Seattle and the Future of Social Movements." *Mobilization* 6, no. 1 (spring 2001): 1–19.

——. "Transnational Political Processes and the Human Rights Movement." *Research in Social Movements, Conflicts and Change* 18 (1995): 185–219.

Smith, Jackie, and Hank Johnston, eds. *Globalization and Resistance: Transnational Dimensions of Social Movements*. New York: Rowman and Littlefield, 2002.

Smith, Michelle. "Potential Solutions to the Problem of Pregnancy Discrimination in *Maquiladoras* Operated by US Employers in Mexico." *Berkeley Women's Law Journal* 13 (1998): 195–225.

Soros, George. *On Globalization*. New York: Public Affairs, 2002.

South Asia Association for Regional Cooperation. "Third SAARC Ministerial Conference on Children, 20–22 August 1996, Rawalpindi: Background Notes." Rawalpindi, Pakistan: UNICEF ROSA, October 1997.

Spivak, Gayatri Chakravorty. *A Critique of Postcolonial Reason: Toward a History of the Vanishing Present*. Cambridge: Harvard University Press, 1999.

Steiner, Henry J., and Philip Alston, eds. *International Human Rights in Context: Law, Politics and Morals*. Oxford: Clarendon Press, 1996.

Stephens, Beth. "The Amorality of Profit: Transnational Corporations and Human Rights." *Berkeley Journal of International Law* 20, no. 1 (2002): 45–90.

——. "Corporate Liability: Enforcing Human Rights through Domestic Litigation." *Hastings International and Comparative Law Review* 24, no. 3 (spring 2001): 401–13.

Stevenson, Linda. "Confronting Gender Discrimination in the Mexican Workplace: Women and Labor Facing NAFTA with Transnational Contention." *Women and Politics* 26, no. 1 (2004): 71–97.

——. "Confronting Gender Discrimination in the Mexican Workplace: Women Taking Action in Local, National and Transnational Policy Arenas." In "Gender Politics and Policy Process in Mexico, 1968–2000: Symbolic Gains for Women in an Emerging Democracy." Ph.D. diss., University of Pittsburgh, 2000.

——. "The Impact of Feminist Civil Society Movements and NGOs on Gender Policies in Mexico." Paper presented at the annual meeting of the American Political Science Association, Chicago, 1–5 September 2004.

Stiglitz, Joseph. *Globalization and Its Discontents*. New York: Norton, 2002.

Stinchcombe, Arthur. "The Conditions of Fruitfulness of Theorizing about Mechanisms in Social Science." In *Social Theory and Social Policy: Essays in Honor of James S. Coleman*, ed. Aage B. Sorensen and Seymour Spilerman, 23–41. Westport, CT: Praeger 1993.

Tarrow, Sidney. "From Lumping to Splitting: Specifying Globalization and Resistance." In *Globalization and Resistance: Transnational Dimensions of Social Movements*, ed. Jackie Smith and Hank Johnston, 229–49. Lanham, MD: Rowman and Littlefield, 2002.

——. *Power in Movement: Social Movements and Contentious Politics*. 2nd ed. Cambridge: Cambridge University Press, 1998.

——. "Social Movements in Contentious Politics: A Review Essay." *American Political Science Review* 90, no. 4 (December 1996): 874–83.

Thomas, Caroline. "International Financial Institutions and Social and Economic Human Rights: An Exploration." In *Human Rights Fifty Years On: A Reappraisal*, ed. Tony Evans, 161–85. Manchester, UK: Manchester University Press, 1998.

Tilly, Charles. *From Mobilization to Revolution*. Reading, MA: Addison-Wesley, 1978.

——. *Popular Contention in Great Britain, 1758–1834*. Cambridge: Harvard University Press, 1995.

Traugott, Marc. *Repertoires and Cycles of Collective Action*. Durham, NC: Duke University Press, 1995.

Tsebelis, George. *Nested Games: Rational Choice in Comparative Politics*. Berkeley: University of California Press, 1990.

United Food and Commercial Workers Union, Women's Network. "Help Stop Child Labor: Don't Buy Clothes Made in Bangladesh Sold at Wal-Mart Stores." Undated flyer. Photocopy on file with the author.

United Nations. "Annotations on the Text of the Draft International Covenants on Human Rights." UN Doc. A/2929 (1955).

——. "Entrenched attitudes must be uprooted for Mexican women to advance, women's anti-discrimination committee told." Press release (WOM/1019), 30 January 1998. Photocopy on file with the author.

——. "Progress made in advancement of Mexican women, but changes not yet 'radical,' anti-discrimination committee told." Press release (WOM/1020), 30 January 1998. Photocopy on file with the author.

——. *Report of the Committee on the Elimination of Discrimination against Women* (Eighteenth and Nineteenth sessions). General Assembly, Official Records, 53rd session, supplement no. 38 (A/53/38/Rev.1).

United Nations Children's Fund (UNICEF). *Assessment of the Memorandum of Understanding regarding Placement of Child Workers in School Programmes and Elimination of Child Labour in the Bangladesh Garment Industry, 1995–2001*. New York: UNICEF, 2004.

——. *Poverty and Children: Lessons of the 90s for Least Developed Countries*. New York: UNICEF, May 2001.

United Nations Children's Fund and ILO/IPEC. *Addressing Child Labour in the Bangladesh Garment Industry, 1995–2001: A Synthesis of UNICEF and ILO Evaluation Studies of the Bangladesh Garment Sector Projects*. New York and Geneva: UNICEF and ILO, August 2004.

United Nations Committee on the Rights of the Child. "Consideration of Reports Submitted by States Parties under Article 44 of the Convention [on the Rights of the Child]." CRC/C/65/Add.22, 14 March 2003. Available electronically via http://www.hri.ca/fortherecord2003/documentation/tbodies/crc-c-65–add22.htm.

——. "Initial Reports of States Parties Due in 1992: Bangladesh. 07/12/95—Consideration of Reports Submitted by States Parties under Article 44 of the Convention [on the Rights of the Child]." CRC/C/3/Add.38, 7 December 1995. Available electronically via http://www.unhchr.ch/tbs/doc.nsf.

——. *Summary Record of the 569th Meeting, Committee on the Rights of the Child, [second periodic report of] Mexico*. Twenty-second session, 27 September 1999 (CRC/C/SR.569), distributed 5 October 1999. Available electronically via http://www.unhchr.ch/tbs/doc.nsf/.

United Nations Development Programme (UNDP). *Human Development Report 2005*. New York: Oxford University Press, 2005.

——. *Human Development Report 1995.* New York: Oxford University Press, 1995.

United Nations Economic and Social Council. "Concluding Observations of the Committee on Economic, Social and Cultural Rights: Mexico 08/12/99." E/C.12/1/Add.41 (Concluding Observations/Comments), 8 December 1999. Available electronically via http://www.unhchr.ch/tbs/doc.nsf/(Symbol)/E.C .12.1.ADD.41.En?Opendocument.

United Nations Nongovernmental Liaison Service. "Jubilee South-South Summit." *Go Between* 78 (December 1999–January 2000): 19.

United States Central Intelligence Agency. *CIA Factbook 2001.* Available electronically via http://www.cia.gov/cia/publications/factbook/.

United States Congress, House of Representatives. "Press Packet on Child Labor Reform Legislation." 18 March 1993. Photocopy on file with the author.

United States Congress, House of Representatives, Office of Representative Tom Harkin. "Harkin Study Confirms Use of Child Labor in US Imports." Press release, 19 September 1994.

United States Congress, House of Representatives, Office of Representative Donald Pease of Ohio. Testimony on child labor cited in *Congressional Record*, 102nd Congress, 1st session, 15 November 1991, vol. 137, part 25.

United States Congress, House of Representatives, Office of Representative George Miller of California. Testimony on child labor cited in *Congressional Record*, 100th Congress, 1st session, 14 July 1987, vol. 133, part 27.

United States Department of Labor, Bureau of International Labor Affairs. *Advancing the Campaign against Child Labor: Efforts at the Country Level.* Washington, DC: US Department of Labor, 2002.

——. *By the Sweat and Toil of Children,* vol. 1: *The Use of Child Labor in US Manufactured and Mined Imports.* Washington, DC: Department of Labor, International Labor Affairs Bureau, 1994.

——. "Labor Department Funds Governments for the Eradication of Child Labor." News release 96–207, 30 May 1996.

United States Department of State, Bureau of Democracy, Human Rights and Labor. "Mexico Country Report on Human Rights Practices for 1999." Released 25 February 2000.

——. "Mexico Country Report on Human Rights Practices for 1998." Released 26 February 1999.

United States National Administrative Office (US-NAO), Bureau of International Labor Affairs, United States Department of Labor. *Public Report of Review of NAO Submission No. 9701.* Dated 12 January 1998. Available electronically via http:// www.dol.gov/ILAB/media/reports/nao/pubrep9701.htm.

——. "Status of Submissions under the North American Agreement on Labor Cooperation," updated 11 January 2000. Available from the US-NAO in photocopy form.

——. "Witnesses, Public Hearing on Submission no. 9701, Brownsville, Texas, 19 November 1997." Undated photocopy, available from the US-NAO.

Valadéz-Prez, Carmen. "Mexico: NAFTA versus Human Rights." In *Women's Lives in the New Global Economy—Notebook for Study and Research,* ed. Penny Duggan and Heather Dashner, 51–55. Notebook for Study and Research no. 22. Amsterdam: International Institute for Research and Education, 1994.

Van Evera, Stephen. *Guide to Methods for Students of Political Science.* Ithaca: Cornell University Press, 1997.

Vázquez-Tercero, Héctor. "Medición de flujo de divisas de la balanza comercial de México." *Comercio Exterior* 40, no. 10 (October 2000): 890–94.

Velasco, Diana. "Despidos por embarazo en la mujer, no se denuncia en 90% de los casos." *El Día*, 21 October 1998.

Weston, Burns H. *Child Labor and Human Rights: Making Children Matter*. Boulder, CO: Lynne Rienner, 2005.

White, Ben. "Children, Work and 'Child Labor': Changing Responses to the Employment of Children." *Development and Change* 25, no. 4 (October 1994): 849–78.

White, Sarah C. "From the Politics of Poverty to the Politics of Identity? Child Rights and Working Children in Bangladesh." *Journal of International Development* 14 (2002): 725–35.

Williams, Heather. "Mobile Capital and Transborder Labor Rights Mobilization." *Politics and Society* 27, no. 1 (March 1999): 139–66.

Yee, Albert S. "The Causal Effects of Ideas on Policies." *International Organization* 50, no. 1 (winter 1996): 69–108.

Zald, Mayer. "Culture, Ideology, and Strategic Framing." In *Comparative Perspectives on Social Movements*, ed. Doug McAdam, John D. McCarthy, and Mayer N. Zald, 261–74. Cambridge: Cambridge University Press, 1996.

Index